THE DEATH OF IVAN ILICH

An Interpretation

TWAYNE'S MASTERWORK STUDIES

Robert Lecker, General Editor

THE DEATH OF IVAN ILICH

An Interpretation

Gary R. Jahn

TWAYNE PUBLISHERS • NEW YORK

Maxwell Macmillan Canada • Toronto
Maxwell Macmillan International • New York Oxford Singapore Sydney

Twayne's Masterwork Studies No. 119

The Death of Ivan Ilich: An Interpretation
Gary R. Jahn

Twayne Publishers   Maxwell Macmillan Canada, Inc.
Macmillan Publishing Company   1200 Eglinton Avenue East
866 Third Avenue   Suite 200
New York, New York 10022   Don Mills, Ontario M3C 3N1

Library of Congress Cataloging-in-Publication Data
Jahn, Gary R.
    The death of Ivan Ilich : an interpretation / Gary R. Jahn.
        p.   cm. — (Twayne's masterwork studies ; no. 119)
    Includes bibliographical references and index.
    ISBN 0-8057-9439-5. — ISBN 0-8057-8583-3 (pbk.)
        1. Tolstoy, Leo, graf, 1828–1910.   Smert' Ivana Il 'icha.
    I. Title. II. Series.
    PG3366.S63J3   1993
    891.73'3—dc20   92-44537
                                                        CIP

The paper used in this publication meets the minimum requirements of American
National Standard for Information Sciences—Permanence of Paper for Printed
Library Materials. ANSI Z3948-1984.∞™

10 9 8 7 6 5 4 3 2 1 (hc)
10 9 8 7 6 5 4 3 2 1 (pb)

Printed in the United States of America

For Katherine and Robert Jahn

CONTENTS

LEO TOLSTOY, about 1885

NOTE ON THE REFERENCES
AND ACKNOWLEDGMENTS

The authoritative, scholarly edition of the works of Leo Tolstoy in Russian is *Polnoe sobranie sochinenii v devianosto tomakh* (Moscow and Leningrad: Gosudarstvennoe Izdatel'stvo Khudozhestvennoi Literatury, 1928–1958). This edition, which contains in excess of 30,000 pages of text and commentary in its 90 volumes, is the most complete single collection of Tolstoy's works (published and unpublished) and private papers. It is often referred to as the "Jubilee Edition" because its publication commenced on the one hundredth anniversary of Tolstoy's birth. The text of *The Death of Ivan Ilich* is printed in volume 26 of this edition. I am indebted to the editors of this volume for the information provided in their commentary on the novel; I have made free use of this information in some of the chapters of this book.

I have selected the translation of *The Death of Ivan Ilich* by Louise and Aylmer Maude as my English text. Of the various editions of this translation currently in print I would steer the reader toward a recently published anthology of Tolstoy's short fiction: *Tolstoy's Short Fiction*, edited and with revised translations by Michael R. Katz (W. W. Norton & Co.: New York, 1991). This volume provides the texts of several of Tolstoy's other shorter works of fiction, including another novel, *Master and Man*, to which I will refer in this book. In addition, the collection is supplemented by a number of scholarly studies of Tolstoy's shorter fiction, including several that are directly relevant to *The Death of Ivan Ilich*. I selected the Maude translation of the novel rather than any of the several others that are available because they were contemporaries of Tolstoy, were indeed close friends of his, and were very much attuned to the spirit of his works, particularly his later writings.

Parenthetic references to the text of *The Death of Ivan Ilich* give the page number(s) of the English text first and then those of the Russian text (e.g., 123 [26:61]). All translations of Russian language material other than the text of the novel itself are my own.

Some of the material in this book has appeared in previous publications. I am grateful to the copyright holders for their permission to use portions, revised for this publication, of my earlier studies: "L. N. Tolstoj's Vision of the Power of Death and 'How Much Land Does a Man Need,' " *Slavic and East European Journal* 22(1978):442–53; "The Unity of *Anna Karenina*," *The Russian Review 41*, no. 2 (April 1982):144–58, Copyright 1982 The Russian Review, Inc. All rights reserved; "The Role of the Ending in Lev Tolstoi's *The Death of Ivan Il'ich*," *Canadian Slavonic Papers* 24(1982):229–38; "*The Death of Ivan Il'ich*—Chapter One," in *Studies in Nineteenth and Twentieth Century Polish and Russian Literature*, ed. Lauren G. Leighton and George Gutsche (Columbus, Ohio: Slavica Publishers, 1983), 37–43; "A Note on Miracle Motifs in the Later Works of Lev Tolstoj," in *The Supernatural in Slavic and Baltic Literatures*, ed. Amy Mandelker and Roberta Reeder (Columbus, Ohio: Slavica Publishers, 1988), 191–99.

I would like to acknowledge with thanks the assistance I have received with various aspects of my research for this book. Pamela Mullen-Schultz and Kelly Wahl helped me in the preparation and cataloging of bibliographical sources. Justin Weir was good enough to share with me his own research into the connections between *The Death of Ivan Ilich* and *On Life*.

There is an enormous secondary literature on Tolstoy and on *The Death of Ivan Ilich*. Only a small portion of it has been used directly in this study, but its oblique influence in shaping my approach to Tolstoy can scarcely be overestimated. I, therefore, make due acknowledgment here to the work of the numerous family of Tolstoy scholars around the world and across the generations.

CHRONOLOGY:
LEO TOLSTOY'S LIFE AND WORKS

1828	Born on 28 August (Old Style), the fourth of five children, into a wealthy aristocratic family residing at a country estate called Yasnaya Polyana (located about 120 miles south and slightly east of Moscow). His father was a retired army officer, his mother a wealthy heiress of the Volkonsky family.
1830	Death of his mother in childbirth.
1837	Sudden death of his father.
1837–1848	Cared for by a succession of female relatives; attends (1844–47) Kazan University, leaving without completing a degree.
1848	Attains his majority and inherits the Yasnaya Polyana estate; Yasnaya Polyana becomes his permanent residence.
1851	Joins his elder brother on active duty with the Russian army in the Caucasus; serves (1851–56) in various theaters of operation and is decorated for bravery.
1852	His first published work, the novel *Childhood*, appears in *The Contemporary*, a leading magazine of the time. An account of selected experiences from the life of a young boy as mediated through the narration of the young hero as an adult, *Childhood* is hailed as a major literary contribution and confers immediate literary significance and prestige upon its author.
1853–1858	Publishes a number of stories, many of them relating to war and army life. Especially well received are the "Sevastopol Stories" (1855–56), three quasi-journalistic accounts of life in the besieged city of Sevastopol during the Crimean war. Publishes two sequels to *Childhood*: *Boyhood* (1854) and *Youth* (1857).
1859	After some three years of literary celebrity in the capital, finds himself completely disillusioned with his calling as a writer.

Leaves St. Petersburg and returns to Yasnaya Polyana, planning to devote himself to estate management and to the establishment of a school for the children of the peasants living on his estate.

1860–1861   Makes a 10-month tour of Europe with the purpose, among others, of studying educational practices in various countries, especially Germany. Following the great governmental reforms of 1861, he is elected "arbiter of the peace" for his district, an office established as part of the increased local autonomy granted by the reforms.

1862   Begins the publication of a magazine, *Yasnaya Polyana*, largely written by himself and devoted to pedagogical questions. (Publication ceases in 1863, after 12 issues have appeared.) Marries Sofia Andreevna Bers, the 17-year-old daughter of a Moscow physician; the marriage, which is often troubled in its later years, lasts until his death and produces 13 offspring, the last in 1888.

1863   Publishes *The Cossacks*, a novel based upon his experiences in the military, and begins working on *War and Peace*, a mammoth novel concerning the period of the Napoleonic wars in Russian history (1805–20).

1869   The publication of *War and Peace* is completed with the appearance of the novel's fifth and sixth volumes.

1870   Following the completion of *War and Peace*, he experiences another period of revulsion for his calling as writer. Once again he turns to educational work.

1872   Publishes his *Primer*, a complete set of materials for elementary education.

1873   Begins writing *Anna Karenina*, the second long novel on which (together with *War and Peace*) his fame as a writer is mainly based. *Anna Karenina*, completed in 1877, concerns the theme of marriage and family life, especially the status of the individual within the context of marriage, family, and society at large.

1875   A period of increasing depression begins, which culminates and is resolved in 1878 with his "conversion" to a version of Christianity. His newfound religious beliefs are mainly of his own devising but have much in common with other radical versions of Christian teaching. He devotes himself from 1878 to 1882 to the writing of a series of works in which he explains his beliefs. Prefaced by the autobiographical *A Confession*, these three works (*A Critique of Dogmatic Theology, A Harmonization and Translation of the Four Gospels,* and *What I*

Believe) are thereafter regarded by Tolstoy as his major achievement as a writer.

1883   Publishes *The Gospel in Brief*, a condensation of *A Harmonization and Translation of the Four Gospels*.

1885   Returns to the writing of fiction with a series of "Stories for the People," brief works intended to convey his religious message to the popular audience. In order to provide an effective means of distributing these and other writings that he regards as morally useful, he founds a publishing house called "The Intermediary." He is assisted in this venture by V. G. Chertkov, later the chief disciple of Tolstoy's teaching. "The Intermediary" is a major success, the first such venture actually to bring large numbers of books to the Russian countryside.

1886   Writes *The Death of Ivan Ilich* (published 1886) and begins a major philosophical treatise, *On Life* (published 1887). The latter is his most complete account of his understanding of the nature and significance of human life and his beliefs with respect to proper human conduct. He remains actively engaged until the end of his life in the promulgation of his religious beliefs. He writes essays and tracts on a variety of social, political, and economic topics (e.g., pacifism, vegetarianism, sexuality, the evils of tobacco and alcohol, capital punishment, anarchism), on art and aesthetics (especially *What Is Art?*, 1898), and further essays on religion. He becomes a cult figure of the time, an object of pilgrimage and veneration. He is hopelessly at odds with the government and the official (Russian Orthodox) church. Nearly all of his writings are either heavily censored or forbidden publication outright; in 1901 he is excommunicated from the Russian Orthodox Church.

1888   Finishes *The Kreutzer Sonata*, a novel celebrated for its radical approach to questions of marriage and sexuality. Not long after, he begins work on his third long novel, *Resurrection*, which he intends as an artistic synthesis of his social and religious views and completes in 1899.

1895   Publishes *Master and Man*. This short novel and *The Death of Ivan Ilich* are usually regarded as the greatest works of the latter half (1880–1910) of Tolstoy's literary career.

1901   Falls seriously ill. Recovers, but the last decade of his life is a time of continuing ill health. Devotes himself to the compilation of anthologies of spiritual wisdom, collections of quotations from the words and writings of noted sages of the past arranged for reading by the day, week, or month. Among these miscellanies are *The Cycle of Reading*, *For Every Day*, and *The Path of Life*.

1910   Following a lengthy period of more or less steady decline in the tranquility and happiness of his domestic life, he abruptly leaves home, accompanied by his youngest daughter and his personal physician. While traveling by train he falls ill and, after clinging to life for several days, dies in the stationmaster's house at the tiny railway station at Astapovo (today the town is called Lev Tolstoy). His body is returned to Yasnaya Polyana and buried there at the edge of a ravine where, in youth, he and his brothers used to play a game, the object of which was to find a mythical "green stick" on which was supposed to be inscribed the secret of human well-being and happiness.

Literary and Historical Context

1

Situating the Text

The accession of Tsar Alexander II to the throne of the Russian empire in 1855 followed by three years the appearance of Leo Tolstoy's first published work and had been celebrated with hopes for a more liberal, more European future for the political life of the nation. These hopes were realized at least in part as Alexander carried through a number of basic reforms in the first half of the 1860s, most notably the emancipation of the serfs (1861). As often happens, a taste of reform became a hunger for reform, a hunger that Alexander in the late 1860s and 1870s was increasingly unwilling to satisfy. Disaffection from the "Tsar-Liberator" culminated in 1881 with his assassination on the streets of St. Petersburg during a royal procession.

Alexander III succeeded his murdered father, determined not to meet a similar fate. Where his father had been educated by the gentle poet Zhukovsky, Alexander III had been tutored by Konstantin Pobedonostsev, a theoretician of archconservatism, who would become one of the new tsar's main advisers and the chief architect of Russia's final renunciation of the liberal promise of the early reign of Alexander II. Many repressive measures were adopted by the government of Alexander III: some university departments were closed for "free-thinking," the censorship of printed materials was strengthened, school curricula were impoverished. Tolstoy's younger contemporary, Anton Chekhov, chronicled the effects of these changes in such stories as "Sergeant Prishibeev" and "The Man in a Shell." He portrays a public life in which the main rule of action is "what is not expressly permitted is forbidden."

Tolstoy brought himself to the unfavorable attention of the new tsar almost at once by writing him an open letter in which he urged Alexander III to set a radically new example for his nation and the world by pardoning the murderers of his father. The tsar refused to grant Tolstoy's request, and, in the years that followed, the tsar's censors refused to permit the publication of works by Tolstoy that expressed in detail the beliefs that had inspired his dramatic plea for royal clemency. These works occupied Tolstoy's attention as a writer almost exclusively in the late 1870s and the early 1880s, and no example of Tolstoy's fiction written in the 1880s or later (including *The Death of Ivan Ilich* [*Smert' Ivana Il'icha*, 1886]) can be fully understood in isolation from the ideas that he presented in them.

Tolstoy was by no means the first to hold the ideas of brotherly love, mutual support, and Christian charity that became so precious to him in the second half of his life; in fact, he came to believe that they were none other than the central tenets of a perennially fresh philosophy of life that had been subscribed to throughout history and in every corner of the earth by the great sages from Socrates to Schopenhauer. No other representative of the "perennial philosophy,"[1] however, has left so clear and vivid an account of the spiritual and psychological travail amidst which his new convictions were born.

In *A Confession* (*Ispoved'*), written mainly in 1879–80 but not completed until 1882, Tolstoy wrote that the factor that before all others prompted the psychological crisis he endured in the mid-1870s (and which is reflected in the character of Konstantin Levin in *Anna Karenina*) was his inability to find an acceptable meaning in human life. Every formulation of life's meaning with which he experimented was wrecked by his long-standing and by now almost overwhelming sense of the dreadful inevitability of death. He writes in *A Confession*: "My life came to a standstill. I could breathe, eat, drink, and sleep, and I could not help doing these things; but there was no life, for there were no wishes, the fulfillment of which I could consider reasonable."[2]

Tolstoy describes several attempts he made to shake off the feelings of depression and despair from which he had increasingly suffered since his first experience of what he called the "Arzamas terror" in 1868[3] (vividly described in his unfinished short story "The Notes of a Madman"). His reading of the great philosophers of the past only confirmed the apparent meaninglessness of life that so troubled him. Turning from his library to his friends and acquaintances for help was also of no avail; either his contemporaries did not concern themselves at all with the questions he found so perplexing or their answers were no more comforting than those given by the philosophers.

Finally, he turned to the broad masses of the Russian people, the peasants, for help. It seemed to him that these illiterate and uneducated folk nevertheless possessed a definite conception of the meaning of life. He wrote in *A Confession* that "it became clear that mankind as a whole had a kind of knowledge, unacknowledged and scorned by me, of the meaning of life . . . They find this meaning in irrational knowledge. And this irrational knowledge is faith, the very same faith [that is, the theology and cult practices of the Russian Orthodox Church] which I could not but reject" (23:32–33).

He saw that the faith of the Russian peasants gave meaning to their lives and protected them from the despair from which he suffered; their faith itself, however, both in its dogma and its cult, had long been abhorrent to him.[4] He seemed to face a choice between a saving, but irrational, faith and the meaningless despair his reason showed him. In the end he reconciled himself to the irrational. "Faith still remained for me as irrational as it was before, but I could not but admit that it alone gives people a reply to the questions of life, and that consequently it makes life possible" (23:35).

He first attempted to renew his connection with the church of his childhood. For a time he carefully and conscientiously observed all the Orthodox rites, but the superstition he detected in that faith, especially as practiced by the peasants whose life he declared otherwise so admirable, soon proved fatal to his resolve. He abandoned the attempt to find a place for himself within the existing system of religion and determined to develop a system of his own. This task occupied him intensively for about four years (1878–1882) and resulted in the preparation of four works that Tolstoy thereafter considered to be his most important achievement. After *A Confession*, which is a brief account and interpretation of his life and moral struggle through the mid-1870s, he wrote *A Critique of Dogmatic Theology (Issledovanie dogmaticheskogo bogosloviia) A Harmony and Translation of the Four Gospels (Soedinenie i perevod chetyrekh evangelii)*, and *What I Believe (V chem moia vera)*. Once completed, these works formed the conscious intellectual center of his thought and action for his remaining 30 years of life.

The central, indeed the only, article of Tolstoy's faith was a belief in the existence of a creator God: "But here I examined myself, examined what was taking place within me; and I recalled all those hundreds of dyings and quickenings which had taken place within me. I recalled that I lived only when I believed in God. As before, so now, I said to myself: 'I need only to know about God, and I live; I need only forget, disbelieve in God, and I die.' I am alive, really alive, only when I sense God and search for God. 'Then for what should I look further?' cried a voice within me. 'That is God. God is that without which it is impossible to live. To know God and to live are one and the same. God is life' " (23:45–46).

Tolstoy's ideas may be seen as one aspect of the turn in Russian intellectual life away from the materialism that had dominated the late 1850s and 1860s and toward a renewed emphasis on spiritual and religious values. The old materialism, however, continued to be philosophically viable, while the renewed spiritualism was sharply fractionated, particularly as between proponents of the traditional religious values and practices of the Orthodox faith and those who, like Tolstoy, rebelled against the teachings of the church. In art and literature the movement away from realism was particularly sharp. The leading trend in literature from about 1890 is called "modernism," a catchall term that subsumes the work of the so-called decadents, the symbolists, and a variety of other groups, which, despite their diversity, shared a distaste for traditional realism. It is interesting that while Tolstoy bitterly attacked the artistic practices of the modernists in his *What Is Art? (Chto takoe iskusstvo?*, 1898), *The Death of Ivan Ilich* is profoundly symbolic and may be seen as a harbinger of the symbolist art that followed in the 1890s and later.

2

The Importance of the Work

Every passing year brings fresh proof of the continuing vitality of Tolstoy's *The Death of Ivan Ilich*. Indeed, the untimely death of Tolstoy's hero seems almost to have been compensated by the longevity of the story memorializing him. What is it that accounts for the continued vitality of this short novel?

Nearly everything that Leo Tolstoy wrote is of considerable interest, since he is one of the giants of Russian literature. *The Death of Ivan Ilich*, however, is regarded as one of his great masterpieces; many would say that it is the chef d'oeuvre of the second half of his literary career. Written in 1886, it was the first major fictional work published by Tolstoy after his crisis and conversion of the late 1870s. For a considerable period after 1878 Tolstoy had turned away from literature altogether in favor of his biblical and theological writings. Thus, it was with considerable interest that the reading public of the mid-1880s learned of the publication of a new novel from the pen of the author of *War and Peace* and *Anna Karenina*.

The novel that they read in the pages of the twelfth (and last) volume of Tolstoy's collected works, subtitled *Works of Recent Years*, surprised many of Tolstoy's old admirers and disappointed others.

The reasons for disappointment were largely ideological. I will discuss the initial reaction to the novel's publication in the next chapter. Here it will suffice to say that it was not long before the novel came to be universally regarded as one of the greatest works of a very great writer.

The Death of Ivan Ilich can be and has been variously interpreted, but it possesses certain basic qualities that must be accounted for in any cogent reading of the novel. It is a devastatingly satirical account of the life of the well-to-do professional class of late-nineteenth-century Russia. In representing the life of a member of this class, Tolstoy shows a masterful (and occasionally uncanny) ability to seize upon the apt situation or detail. The novel is a remarkable example of realism, but at the same time it contains many anticipations of the symbolist art that would shortly (during the 1890s and the first decade of the twentieth century) begin to predominate in Russian literature. Finally, the novel is exemplary of Tolstoy's postconversion philosophical concerns and revised understanding of the mission of art and of the artist.

These qualities, however, could hardly account, by themselves, for the continuing power of *The Death of Ivan Ilich* to seize and hold the imagination of its readers. The English poet and critic Matthew Arnold once said of Tolstoy (referring to the novel *Anna Karenina*) that he created not art, but life itself.[1] Tolstoy was a master of representation and verisimilitude. His characters, and the situations in which they find themselves, seem to come alive to the point that readers often feel as though they know Tolstoy's characters as well as or better than some actual acquaintances. In addition, the particular dimension of life that Tolstoy addresses in *The Death of Ivan Ilich* is one of inescapable interest to all readers. His basic subject is the inevitable confrontation of a human being with her or his own mortality, the coming to grips with the certainty that our lives will end. It is one of Tolstoy's major contentions in the novel that people are, in general, very adept at hiding this ultimate truth from themselves, and he spares no effort in his determination to "remove the coverings" with which we attempt to mask the figure of death in our consciousness.

The importance of the novel for the general reader, then, is that it provides a keenly observed and unsparingly realistic account of a moment in life that we shall all experience; as the character Gerasim says in chapter 1 of the novel, "We will all come to it one day." Aside, then, from the elegance of its structure, the apparent simplicity and directness of its style, and the authenticity and acuity of its observation of a form of life that seems still rather familiar in the 1990s, the novel impresses the reader with the seriousness of its purpose and its moral earnestness, and above all with the evident applicability of the life and death of its protagonist to each reader individually.

3

Critical Reception

The critical reaction that greeted the appearance of *The Death of Ivan Ilich*,[1] strange as it may seem given the novel's title, paid little attention to the theme of death. Contemporary critics were more concerned with matters of style and of ideology. Thus, the populist critic N. K. Mikhailovsky, while noting that the novel was a "fine story," also declared that it was "not of the first rank in artistic beauty, in strength or clarity of thought, or finally in the fearless realism of the writing."[2] The response of a certain Lisovsky was more positive—"the story is without parallel in Russian literature and should be acknowledged a triumph of realism and truth in poetry"—but still confined to generalities.[3] The various camps in Russian literary criticism and appreciation had been arrayed in ideologically adversarial groups at least since the time of V. G. Belinsky (the founder of modern Russian literary criticism) in the 1840s.

Works of literature were generally presumed to have an ideological or, at least, broadly educational function, and much of the literary comment of the time consisted of estimates of the degree to which a given author or a given work had succeeded in the fictional or poetic promotion of one or another ideological agenda. Once Tolstoy's fame had spread to Europe, stimulated there by the high praise accorded to his work in *Le Roman Russe* (*The Russian Novel*) by Vicomte Melchior de Vogué,[4] one finds occasional responses to the novel there also. Again, however, these tend toward evaluative generalities. The early history of the novel's reception makes it quite clear, at least, that Tolstoy's contemporaries were much struck by the novel; by and large, the novel was read as an unflattering commentary on the moral shortcomings of the life-style of the privileged classes rather than as a reflection on the common mortality of all people.

Modern criticism and scholarship of *The Death of Ivan Ilich* for the most part no longer consider themselves obliged to deal with the question of the literary value of the novel.[5] Considering the question of value as settled, commentators have devoted themselves to the consideration of specific aspects of the novel's themes and ideas on one hand and its organization and artistic strategies on the other.

THEMES AND IDEAS

Social Issues An early avenue of approach to the novel was to consider it as an attack upon the empty and valueless life of its protagonist and the privileged society of which he was a part. This has been a main theme within Soviet criticism, which, generally speaking, has venerated Tolstoy as an exemplary practitioner of "critical realism." This term denotes a style in literature that, while perhaps not informed by a "proper" (i.e., Marxist) understanding of the human universe, has at least been capable of arriving at "correct" (i.e., negative) judgments upon precommunist forms of social organization. It has been mainly used to describe the practices of such giants of nineteenth-century Russian literature as Gogol, Turgenev, and (certain aspects of) Dostoyevski, besides Tolstoy. From such a point of view *The Death of Ivan Ilich* is without doubt an exemplary text. The life of the protagonist is that of an educated, relatively prosperous, and, above all, ordinary member of the privileged classes of the latter part of the nineteenth century, and the entire direction of the narrative is toward the display of the falseness, insincerity, insensitivity, and consequent spiritual inadequacy of that life. The *History of Russian Literature in Three Volumes*, published by the Soviet Academy of Sciences in 1964, puts it this way: "With profound artistry Tolstoy brands the petty, selfish motives, the insincerity and lies which form the basis of the 'pleasant and decent' life of the privileged members of the gentry and the state bureaucracy"; or again "Leo Tolstoy's merciless satire manifests itself in all its power in *The Death of Ivan Ilich*. Ivan Ilich's friends, even at his graveside, continue to lie and to pretend. . . . The author pitilessly tears the masks from [the faces of his characters], revealing what they really think and feel."[6] It certainly cannot be cogently maintained that the novel does *not* do these things; one may well wonder, however, whether the novel does these things in order to reveal the inadequacy of the social structure implicated in the narrative or whether that inadequacy is revealed as part of some other, larger literary enterprise.

Non-Soviet readers, too, have often drawn attention to the novel's critique of society. The materialism of nineteenth-century bourgeois society, or its twentieth-century counterpart, has been found either responsible for or productive of Ivan Ilich's malaise and alienation. His physiological sickness is read as an indicator of the diseased quality of his life in society and/or of that society itself.[7] The novel has also been taken as a revelation of the manner in which society or "the social" acts as a hindrance to the discovery of the truths every person requires as an individual. In this reading the novel is the narrative of the individual's inevitable separation from the social as the "truth" perceived by the dying protagonist becomes ever more opaque to those surrounding him.[8]

Psychological Issues Most commentators on the novel have declared that Tolstoy is a masterful observer of human psychology; their admiration has been particularly occasioned by such scenes as the conversation among the deceased's colleagues or that between Ivan's wife and Peter Ivanovich. In both of these passages from chapter 1 of the novel the true motives and feelings of the participants are revealed as Tolstoy strips away the masks of sympathy and condolence that they wear. The text provides such an abundance of similar examples that it may well be taken as a revelation of the psychological masking and hypocrisy characteristic of Ivan and his associates' layer of society. In this sense Tolstoy's talent for psychological observation is understood to be employed in the furtherance of the social criticism discussed earlier.

Some scholars have understood the psychological dimension of the novel to be of primary, rather than ancillary, importance. Thus, Boris Sorokin draws our attention to Ivan's habit of psychological "encapsulization." By this is meant Ivan's habit of retreating from the unpleasantnesses of life, principally, of course, from death. The protagonist's retreats from actual reality into a controlled, internal, purely psychological (but, of course, false) reality, which he gradually establishes for himself as he ages, result, in the end, in his isolation from actuality (Sorokin, 295). William Edgerton sees the life of Ivan Ilich becoming a form of death from this isolation.[9] This view of psychology in the novel accounts for the behavior of Ivan Ilich on general, human grounds rather than as a psychopathy occasioned by a particular social environment.

A third approach to psychology in the novel has been along medical or quasi-medical lines. There was at one time (around the turn of the century) some interest in attempting a diagnosis of the illness from which Ivan suffers and eventually dies,[10] despite the fact that it is rather clear in the novel that the exact nature of Ivan's physiological disease is beside the point; his spiritual well-being is the main issue. Yet the basis of this early "medical" criticism, wherein the fictional account is viewed as an actual clinical record, has persisted in certain psychological studies of the novel. James Bartell, for example, applies the theories of Otto Rank and Arthur Janov to the case of Ivan Ilich. He finds the material of the novel suitable for his purposes both on the grounds of its general fit with Rank's and Janov's explanation of the origins of neurosis in the fear of separation/rejection (one manifestation of which is the fear of death) and on the grounds of the presence in the text of the lengthy retrospective analysis of his own life, which Ivan undertakes and which leads to his ultimate escape from "that which was oppressing him." Bartell understands this as a clear anticipation of the therapy suggested by Rank and Janov.[11] Y. J. Dayananda's work on the novel shares the same sort of concern with the material, but he focuses his attention on Ivan's story as an anticipation (and corroboration) of modern research on the psychological stages involved in death and dying. He discovers analogues in the novel to each of the five stages isolated by Elisabeth Kübler-Ross in her *On Death and Dying*: (1) denial and isolation; (2) anger; (3) bargaining; (4) depression; (5) acceptance.[12] Such interpretations as these clearly indicate that Tolstoy's powers of psychological observation were very acute, but it may well be that they are just as much curiosities in the history of the novel's criticism as are the earlier "diagnostic" analyses.

George Gutsche's analysis of the novel, although psychological in its emphasis, proceeds from an entirely different assumption; the hero's story is not seen as material for psychological analysis, but rather a psychological viewpoint is adopted because it seems to offer insight into the novel. Gutsche claims, very cogently, that Ivan Ilich's story is that of a man who comes gradually, and painfully, to the awareness that his perception of the world (his psychological foundations, as it were) has been in error. Tolstoy's novel traces the arduous path followed by the protagonist in his progress toward rectification of these errors of perception.

Philosophical Issues It is entirely in accord with Tolstoy's own interest in philosophy, religion, and ethics that much of the criticism on the novel can be included under this heading. Furthermore, there can be no strict separation between the social criticism (discussed earlier) offered by the novel and the ethical teachings it seems to offer.

Tolstoy's main concern in philosophy was undoubtedly with ethics: the distinction between right and wrong (good and evil) actions. Many commentators direct our attention to the novel as an account of a life wrongly lived and of the protagonist's ultimate realization of its wrongness. Philip Rahv compares the life of Ivan Ilich to that of Joseph K. of Franz Kafka's *The Trial*. In both works it is the protagonists' certainty that their lives have been *well* lived that is the root of their inability to deal with the situations in which they find themselves. Sorokin (500) and Charles Glicksberg[13] both suggest that a major cause for the wrongness of the *manner* of Ivan Ilich's life is his misapprehension of the *nature* of his life. Ivan overlooks the spiritual dimension of his life and the need for faith, and these are shown to be the only antidotes for the oppressive fear of death. Ivan's incorrect understanding of the nature of the moral situation in which he finds himself leads him further and further into a state of unreality; thus, his striving for a life of illusory material reality is at the expense of his life of genuine spiritual reality (Sorokin, 487–88).

The same theme of the irreality of the life of Ivan Ilich is taken up by Geoffrey Clive in his discussion of the "inauthentic." Although his attention is focussed on moral questions, Clive, like some of the psychologically oriented critics mentioned earlier, in effect identifies the novel as being concerned mainly with social criticism. He depicts Ivan Ilich's inauthentic life as the product of the inauthentic (by which is meant *insincere*) behavior that is characteristic of Ivan Ilich's social milieu.[14] The constant practice of inauthentic behavior toward others results, at last, in a lack of truthfulness to the self and a futile attempt to conceal from oneself the significance of life's major occasions, especially death (Clive, 114–17). James Olney adds to this that what Clive would call "authentic" behavior is modeled in the story in the character of the servant Gerasim.[15] Associated with Clive's ideas, but along a different axis of development from that selected by Olney, are the several studies that delineate the roots of existential thought in the novel. Ivan's situation in life is seen as featureless and deprived of meaning and he himself as subject to a steadily increasing sense of alienation. Lev Shestov (now regarded as one of the founders of existential thought) commented at length on the novel (Shestov, 116–27). William Barrett, who regards the novel as "a basic scripture of existentialist thought" (Barrett, 143), has indicated points of comparison between the novel and the writings of both Kierkegaard and Nietzsche (Barrett, 144). Irving Halperin has developed the connection with Kierkegaard, especially with the Danish philosopher's *Sickness unto Death*.[16]

John Donnelly's article on *The Death of Ivan Ilich* bespeaks the concerns of the philosopher more than those of the literary scholar. His work is primarily a discussion of his own view of morality and is more an occasion for his own reflections than an attempt to illuminate the novel. Mainly at issue is what Donnelly regards as the inappropriately (because unrealistically) absolute moral tone of the novel.[17] In a certain sense, Donnelly's essay is akin in spirit to those by Dayananda and Bartell, which also, in their own way, regard the novel more as a source of exemplary matter than as a text in need of interpretation. *The Death of Ivan Ilich* has often been used in this way also by linguists (e.g., the various studies of Barlas) on the grounds that it offers a conveniently sized specimen of the conversational language of educated speakers of the period. The purpose of such studies is, however, openly linguistic, and it is made quite clear that the intention is to use rather than comment upon the text of the novel.[18]

Not as much as one might expect has been made of Tolstoy's religious views as a background to the understanding of *The Death of Ivan Ilich*.[19] Glicksberg (83) explains Tolstoy's failure to "develop to the full" the awful irony of death as a function of his belief in "redemption." In terms of Tolstoy's religious beliefs *redemption* would refer to the individual's freedom to select and his or her actually selecting the spiritual dimension of life as superior to the physiological. Richard Gustafson's recent book *Leo Tolstoy: Resident and Stranger* considers the novel in the context of the theological teaching of the Russian Orthodox church concerning suffering and sin. He suggests that here, as elsewhere, Tolstoy was closer to church teaching than his many militant statements to the contrary would suggest. Thus, suffering is portrayed as the way to self-understanding, almost as a divine kindness to the lost soul of Ivan Ilich. Ivan's illness is discussed as a metaphor for his misapprehension of the nature of human life, or "sin," to use Gustafson's term.[20] Gustafson's treatment of the novel is informed by a comprehensive knowledge of the contents of Tolstoy's religious writings and by a preference for what these writings may suggest as opposed to what they seem to say. A more straightforward link between Tolstoy's religious writings and *The Death of Ivan Ilich* has been suggested by W. R. Hirschberg, who has drawn attention especially to the treatise *On Life* (especially chapter 9), which Tolstoy wrote immediately after *The Death of Ivan Ilich*.

STRUCTURE AND STYLE

The general artistic organization of the novel, its artistic structure, has occasioned considerable critical comment. Halperin was one of the first to point out the steady narrowing of narrative focus in the text. He associates this feature with the portion of the text that recounts Ivan's life after his fall from the ladder. The narrative focus becomes most concentrated at the very end of the novel (Halperin, 337–39). The disproportion of space assigned to Ivan's life before he became ill (about one-fourth of the text) and his illness and death (about three-fourths of the text) has been noted by Olney, who explains this feature as an indication that Ivan's death is much more significant than his life (Olney, 108–9). This topic will receive further attention later on in this book.

In considering the artistic organization of the story, considerable interest has been taken in the question of the placement of the material contained in the first chapter of the novel. Put simply, it has been seen as somewhat problematical that, while the vast majority of the text is devoted to a chronological account of the life and death of the protagonist, the material in chapter 1 pertains to the period after Ivan's death. In terms of the primarily chronological narrative this material seems to belong at the end of the novel rather than at the beginning. C. J. G. Turner has suggested that the placement of the material in the first chapter may be explained by the history of the novel's creation: Tolstoy's original plan had been to tell the story through the device of Ivan's personal diary account of his experiences. The first chapter was to offer an opportunity for this diary to come into the hands of one of the characters (the one who later became Ivan's friend and colleague, Peter Ivanovich) and thence to the reader. Turner also notes that the linguistic structure of chapter 1 is similar to that of chapter 2, which in fact follows it, but would be in strident contrast to that of chapter 12, which would precede it if the material in chapter 1 were placed chronologically.[21] Gunter Schaarschmidt commented on this point more extensively in his analysis of the language of the novel.

The placement of the material in the first chapter is one of a number of questions that have to do with what we may call the "narrative strategy." Edward Wasiolek has commented on this topic at some length. He has suggested that the placement of Ivan's death at the beginning of the text alienates the reader's sympathies from the very outset by providing a sharply critical portrait of those who survive

Ivan Ilich and, by implication, of the sort of life that the decedent had lived (Wasiolek, 324).

Wasiolek is mainly concerned to address a primary criticism of the novel—namely, that its narrative is arbitrary and its narrator intrusive. Wasiolek points out that the basis of such a criticism is in what he calls the "Jamesian fictional imperative." By this is meant that the unfriendly critic has invoked criteria that may be very appropriate to a consideration of the work of Henry James (who is on record as being no admirer of Tolstoy) but very inappropriate to a consideration of a work by Tolstoy (Wasiolek, 318). Wasiolek admits that by the Jamesian standard the narrative strategy of the novel seems arbitrary or "arranged"; it is clear that Tolstoy is intent upon interpreting as well as telling the events portrayed in the novel. Authorial intrusion is part of Tolstoy's narrative stance; if the novel is approached with a prejudice against such a strategy, naturally only an unfavorable judgment of the work is possible (Wasiolek, 317). Wasiolek describes Tolstoy's technique as a "clear and unambiguous control of the meaning he intends" (Wasiolek, 319). This acknowledgment of the importance of considering the author's intentions, at least with an author like Tolstoy, is a most important concept in dealing with *The Death of Ivan Ilich*.

The undisguised presence of Tolstoy the author as an interpreting and guiding force in the narrative has been confirmed by the discovery of a variety of subtexts within the novel. A subtext may take various forms, most commonly that of a pattern of allusions to some other text (either by the same or another author) or a pattern within the narrative that seems to be at odds with the pattern on the surface of the narrative. There will be further discussion of subtext in this second meaning later in this book. Of the first sort of subtext (which has also been called *intertext*) some mention will be made in the last chapter of this book, in the discussion of the role played by this work in the context of Tolstoy's many attempts to deal with the theme of death in his writings. David Matual has considered one particular subtext at length: the intertextual relationship between *The Death of Ivan Ilich* and Tolstoy's *A Confession*, written some half-dozen years earlier. Matual has displayed numerous parallels between the situation of

Tolstoy, as described in *A Confession*, and that of Ivan Ilich, as described in the novel.[22] The effect of the discovery of such a subtext is, of course, that a reading of Ivan's physiological illness as symbolic of underlying spiritual malaise becomes easier to defend and seems more likely to be appropriate.

As we conclude this brief survey of critical comment on the novel, let us turn to the question of the use of image, symbol, metaphor, and other literary figures in the text. This subject will be discussed again later on in this book. It was mentioned in chapter 1 that Tolstoy was very much at odds with the symbolist writers of the 1890s and early 1900s on the grounds that their art was exclusive and unconcerned with the ethical questions Tolstoy considered so important. It is a curious irony that Tolstoy's works, to some extent, prefigure, in their use of symbol and metaphor, some of the aesthetic devices of those later writers whom he would soon be so roundly denouncing. To prevent any misunderstanding, however, it needs to be said that Tolstoy's symbolism is of what we might call a *metonymic* sort: it is based in the use of one report of experience to comment upon, reflect, foreshadow, or explain another experience. Characteristic of the symbolists, however, is a *metaphorical* symbolism, wherein a report of experience on one plane of existence is taken to reflect, explain, etc., experience on a different plane.[23]

Already in *Anna Karenina* (from the mid-1870s) Tolstoy had written a book that many have found to contain profoundly symbolic (in the metonymic sense) elements. The chapter describing the horse race in which Vronsky competes or the scene of Levin mowing hay with the peasants come immediately to mind. In *The Death of Ivan Ilich* this tendency is much intensified. Situations, details, even turns of phrase seem full of meaning and suggestiveness for the reader's understanding of the life and death of the protagonist. Various critics have explained the symbolism of the card game that Ivan is so fond of playing, of his interest in the furnishing of his apartment, of the ladder from which he falls, and of the position he adopts upon the couch in his study. Rima Salys has a thorough discussion of such usages in the novel. George Gutsche's is the best general summary account of the artistry of Tolstoy's use of language, especially of the patterned repetition of key words and phrases and of the play with prefixes, roots, and suffixes in the text.

By far the greatest amount of attention has been paid to the image of the "black bag" or "black hole," which plays so prominent a role in the last four chapters of the novel. Matual has pointed out that this key image is one of the connections between *The Death of Ivan Ilich* and *A Confession*, in which the image first appeared as a "black spot" (Matual, 126). In the main, critics have regarded this image as suggestive of the uterus and as part of the symbolic depiction of Ivan's rebirth (Halperin; Olney). However, Sorokin has elaborated a solid case for the idea that the symbolic referent of the black bag is the bowel, especially in the many references to the caecum (the "blind gut," the appendix) in the text. In either case, and we shall have more to say of this topic in particular in a later chapter, the reader's attention is drawn to the conclusion that the entire account of Ivan Ilich's life and death is symbolically referential, that his physiological life symbolizes his spiritual life. The conclusion has been drawn by Edgerton that Ivan's death is a door to genuine life and that his life had been a form of death (300).

A recent study by Salys has drawn further attention to the suggestively referential use of detail and phrase, specifically to the use of foreign language phrases and common expressions in the novel. The careful reader will notice that there are a number of these: *respice finem* ("look to the end") and *phénix de la famille* ("the phoenix of the family") from chapter 2 of the novel, for example. Salys demonstrates how Tolstoy uses these cliché expressions with suggestive effect in telling and foretelling Ivan's advance along the "road of life."[24]

In this chapter I have introduced the main trends in the scholarship and criticism about *The Death of Ivan Ilich*. Many of the ideas mentioned here will reappear in the chapters that follow. The history of the scholarship and criticism of a notable work of literature is rather like a lengthy discussion. In order to understand any new contribution to such a history one needs to be aware of the context in which it is offered and to which it responds, just as one needs to know in a discussion what the participants have talked about so far if one is to assess the meaning and the significance of any new contribution. In this chapter, then, we have been orienting ourselves to the main themes that have emerged in the discussion of *The Death of Ivan Ilich*. Later we will turn to the text in a detailed consideration that has been nurtured by this discussion and, I hope, contributes positively to it. First, however, some general background to the writing of the text and some preliminary observations about it are in order.

A Reading

4

Background Observations
and General Considerations

Biographical Information

The Death of Ivan Ilich was the product of a time in Tolstoy's life full of hope and anxiety. The years 1885 and 1886 brought death into Tolstoy's house and serious illness to Tolstoy. In December 1885, he wrote (although he never sent the letter) to his friend and disciple, V. G. Chertkov: "I am living through what are perhaps the final hours of my life, and living badly—mournful and irritated with those around me. I am doing something that is not as God would have it; I try to find out what it is, but it eludes me. And always there is this constant anxiety, mournfulness, and worst of all, irritation and the desire for death" (85:294). If the essence of Tolstoy's conversion in the 1870s had been the elaboration of an answer to the question posed by the ineluctable and nullifying power of death, these remarks of the mid-1880s suggest that that answer, which had until then "made life possible" for Tolstoy, was losing its power to persuade. Despite this, or perhaps because of it, these years also saw the creation of many of Tolstoy's most affirmative fictions (the majority of his *Stories for the People* were written in 1885 and 1886) and of *On Life*, his most detailed statement of his views on the positive potential of human existence.

The surface of Tolstoy's story about the life and death of Ivan Ilich seems to reflect more clearly the anxious rather than the hopeful side of the author as he was in the years 1885 and 1886. It will be the general contention of the present monograph that a full appreciation of the novel entails the penetration of that surface and an exploration of the implications it suggests. The purpose of this chapter, however, is to describe how it was that the novel came to be written, to provide background information concerning Tolstoy's conception of art and of the mission of the artist, and to offer some preliminary observations on the organization of the text.

THE COMPOSITION OF THE NOVEL

Tolstoy worked intensively on the novel from August 1885 to March 1886. In a letter to his friend D. Urusov (22 August 1885) Tolstoy refers to "an account of the simple death of a simple man, told from his own point of view" (26:681). Tolstoy's active interest in this subject can be traced back to July or August 1881, when he first heard of the recent (2 July 1881) death of a certain Ivan Ilich Mechnikov, a prosecutor in the regional court of Tula Government (the major subsidiary regions in the administrative organization of Russia were called "governments"; these, in turn, were subdivided into "districts"). Tolstoy knew and liked Mechnikov, about whose death he learned from the deceased's brother, Il'ia Ilich. Mechnikov, who was known as a kindly and benevolent man, served as the partial prototype of Ivan Ilich Golovin, the protagonist of *The Death of Ivan Ilich*. Tolstoy's sister-in-law, Tatyana Kuzminskaya, states in her memoirs that she repeated to Tolstoy what had been confided to her by the deceased's widow, that Mechnikov's dying thoughts had been of the "uselessness of the life which he had lived."[1]

Tolstoy took no immediate action on the impressions aroused by Mechnikov's death. He seems to have left them to develop without conscious supervision in some quiet corner of his reflecting mind; in the period between his first knowledge of the incident and August 1885, only twice is he known to have mentioned a continuing interest in the topic (April and December 1884).

Once Tolstoy had actively set to work on the novel, however, he involved himself in it intensely. He completed a finished draft of the story in January 1886 and sent it to the publisher late in that month or early in February; the proof sheets were returned to him for correction in mid-February; Tolstoy heavily revised these and submitted what was essentially a new version of the novel in early March. Tolstoy further revised the new set of proofs, which he received in mid-March. These corrected proofs, the novel's final revision, were returned to the publisher on 25 March. The novel was first published in volume 12 (the final volume) of *The Works of Count L. N. Tolstoy* later in 1886.

TOLSTOY ON ART AND AS ARTIST

In defining artistic unity Tolstoy paid scant attention to the traditional methods of linkage for which his critics were perhaps looking. In his "Preface to the Works of Guy de Maupassant" ("Predislovie k sochineniiam Giui de Mopassana," 1894) he wrote:

> People who have little artistic sensibility often think that the unity of a work of art depends upon its portraying the actions of a single set of characters or being organized around a single set of complicating circumstances or describing the life of a single person. This is incorrect. . . . The cement which joins any work of art into a unified whole and thus produces the illusion of life is not the unity of characters and situations but rather the unity of the author's own moral relationship to his subject. . . . Therefore, a writer who lacks a clear, definite, and original view of the world . . . cannot produce a work of art. (30:18–19)

As is so often the case, this pronouncement of the old Tolstoy has roots in his youth. Already in 1853 he had written: "In reading a composition, especially a purely literary one, the main interest is the author's character as revealed in the composition. There are compositions in which the author makes an affectation of his view or changes it several times. The best are those wherein the author tries, as it were, to conceal his personal view while always remaining true to it wherever it shows through. The most colorless are those in which the view is so inconsistent as virtually to be lost" (46:182).

The "character of the author," his "view," is his understanding of reality. It is this understanding that determines his moral relationship to his subject. For Tolstoy art was primarily a means of communicating the author's understanding of the nature of reality. The "reality" in which the characters live and act is devised by the author to reflect his understanding of the nature of the reality in which *he* lives and acts. The unifying effect of the author's consistency in applying his insight to the separate fates of the diverse creations of his imagination is the basis of the wholeness of the literary work of art; matters of organizational technique and artistic device are of secondary importance. In part 5 of the novel *Anna Karenina* the heroine, Anna, and her lover, Vronsky, call upon the painter Mikhailov in his studio. A true artist, Mikhailov echoes Tolstoy's impatience with questions of technique and is compared very favorably with the dilettante Vronsky, who is a master of such matters. Mikhailov's portrait of Anna displays her as she really is by "removing the covers" that obscure her true nature (19:42). This suggests that the mission of art, for Tolstoy, is to express reality as it has been revealed to the artist. The substance of Tolstoy's remarks about the unity of a work of literary art, then, is that it is to be found on the thematic level. Its form will be that of an underlying conception of the nature of reality and its function will be to unite the diverse and occasionally contradictory fates of the characters as they participate in that reality.

It would be shortsighted, however, to ignore other factors that contribute to the work's unity. To say that Mikhailov, in the example from *Anna Karenina* just given, attaches minimal value to technique in art is not to say that his work lacks (or that the work of a genuine artist may lack) technical mastery. A brilliant example of Tolstoy's technical skill in the organization of an artistic text is the novel *Anna Karenina* itself.[2]

Background Observations and General Considerations

PRELIMINARY OBSERVATIONS ON THE TEXT

The text of *The Death of Ivan Ilich* runs to about 15,000 words and is divided into 12 chapters. The text is apportioned among these as follows (measured in lines of type):

chapter 1	301	chapter 5	139	chapter 9	93
chapter 2	290	chapter 6	102	chapter 10	72
chapter 3	253	chapter 7	153	chapter 11	96
chapter 4	255	chapter 8	234	chapter 12	73

Roughly speaking, the chapters are organized in a pattern of decreasing length, and, without putting too fine a point on it, it is possible to speak of long (250–300 lines), medium (140–150 lines), and short (70–95 lines) chapters. Besides the general pattern of decreasing length, then, the visual appearance of the text also suggests a division into three parts: chapters 1 through 4, which are all "long" chapters; 5 through 8, of which 5 and 7 are "medium" chapters, 6 a long "short" chapter, and 8 a short "long" chapter; and 9 through 12, which are all "short" chapters.

These data take on added significance when considered in the light of the chapters' contents. Following the introductory material provided in chapter 1, chapters 2 through 4 give an account of the life of Ivan Ilich from his childhood, through the development of his career in government service and his marriage, to the onset of his illness: a period of more than 40 years. Chapters 5 through 8 present the development of the illness, Ivan's further attempts to deal with it, and his growing awareness of the approach of death: a period of several months. The last four chapters recount the hero's final decline and agonized death: a period of a bit more than four weeks. Thus, the decreasing size of the chapters is matched by a parallel decrease in their time frame: from years to months to weeks. The last chapter makes this gradual focusing still more apparent by shrinking the temporal framework from weeks to days, then to hours, and finally brings the flow of time to a stop altogether in the "one changeless instant" in which Ivan finds himself following his illumination.

There is a parallel decrease in the spatial dimensions of the story. Chapters 2 through 4 present the protagonist in the broad context of his official peregrinations from town to town and conclude by localizing him in the city to which his final promotion sends him and in the stylish apartment that he engages there. Chapters 5 through 8 curtail this spatial mobility, and Ivan is ultimately confined to his study. The process is completed in chapters 9 through 12 as the comparative freedom of the study is reduced to the limits of the sofa (chapter 10) on which he dies. Thus, the temporal and spatial stages of the narrative coincide with the three groups of chapters. The gradual contraction of time and space around Ivan Ilich leads logically to the story's time line reaching time-zero and its space line reaching space-zero at the moment of his death.

This brief analysis of the story's surface text indicates the basis for a commonly made criticism of the novel. On one hand the text prepares the reader to accept time-zero and space-zero as points of termination. On the other hand, when time- and space-zero are finally reached in chapter 12, they are, apparently unexpectedly, revealed to be a new beginning, as is shown by Ivan's sense of relief and well-being, his overcoming of time, and his escape from the confines of the "black hole" into a space that contains no dimensions at all, but only light.

The linearity and gradually increasing tempo of the text prepare the reader for a conclusion very like that which Ivan Ilich imagines when he describes his life as "a series of increasing sufferings" that "flies faster and faster towards its end, the most terrible suffering" (163 [26:109]). The astonishing, last-minute reversal that the reader is offered instead has struck some readers as incredible or artistically unjustified. This is not so much a matter of religious convictions as of artistic consistency.

To appreciate the fitness of the ending we must consider the text in the light of the several subtexts embedded within it. To that task we next turn. The next several chapters amount to a running commentary on the novel. I have organized the material, mainly, in accordance with the apparent division of the story into three main sections, as discussed earlier.

5

The Problem of Chapter 1

The purpose of this chapter and the next is to provide a commentary on the first four chapters of *The Death of Ivan Ilich*, the portion of the novel that presents the life of the protagonist from his childhood through the onset of the illness to which he falls victim in his forties. My intention is to provide explanation of difficulties in the text and to draw the reader's attention to points of thematic or artistic significance. The first difficulty of the text is the problematical placement of the material in chapter one.

Among the numerous disputes generated by this "most simple and ordinary story" is the problem of the author's placement of the matter related in the first chapter. Since the remainder of the work contains not a single departure from strict chronological order in its account of the protagonist's life and death, some have found it strange that the story's chronologically final chapter should have been placed first.

The question evoked by the narrative displacement of the account in chapter 1 of the public announcement of Ivan's demise, its effect on his judicial colleagues and family, and Peter Ivanovich's attendance at the requiem for his deceased friend has been stated by C. J. G. Turner:

"Why is this chapter there at all, and why is it placed at the beginning of the story rather than at the end?" (Turner, 120). According to Turner, the first chapter, as we have it, is a relic of an earlier, eventually discarded, plan for telling the story. Even so, he continues, it manages to retain a reasonably justifiable function in the final text: "The chronological displacement of this chapter enables it to suggest, by its structural position at the beginning of the story, the social milieu in which Ivan Ilyich was to make his career and at the same time, by its chronological position at the end of the story, the fact that the milieu was unchanged when his career came to an end" (Turner, 121). Such is certainly the suggestion of the ironic presentation of the reactions of those close to the protagonist to his death and is especially clear in the portrait of the "profound sorrow" of Ivan's widow, Praskovya Fyodorovna. The scene in which she receives the condolences of Peter Ivanovich is marked not only by the conventionality and insincerity of her sorrow but also by the completely materialistic nature of her present concerns: how to deal with the undertaker and the cemetery in the most economical fashion and how to maximize her return from her husband's pension. These concerns with material things are echoed with cutting humor by references to the power of certain objects: the bright, unmarred surface of the little table, which Praskovya Fyodorovna makes haste to protect from Peter Ivanovich's cigarette ash; the black lace of the widow's shawl, which becomes caught on the ornately carved edge of the table; the rebellious "pouffe" (a small upholstered hassock or stool) whose resilient and squeaky springs cause Peter Ivanovich so much embarrassment (127 [26:67]).[1]

Gunter Schaarschmidt, however, maintains that Turner's opinion does insufficient justice to the structural integrity of the story's final version (Schaarschmidt, 356–66). He identifies a tension between inert habit and dawning awareness as the thematic dominant of the story, and he maintains that this tension is revealed even in the pattern of the story's organization. He divides the text into three parts: (1) chapter 1, (2) chapters 2 and 3, and (3) chapters 4 through 12 (Schaarschmidt, 358–60). A gradual shift from "awareness" to "habit" is evident in the first section, the second section is dominated by "habit," while the third presents a gradual shift from "habit" to "awareness" (Schaarschmidt, 365). The extrachronological positioning of the first chapter thus results in an organization that is analogous to a mirror image: awareness to habit—habit—habit to awareness. This symmetry is not possible on the basis of a purely chronological organization, and Schaarschmidt justifiably concludes that "to say that chapter one could be transposed so easily to the end is to ignore that so doing creates a narrative hiatus between the end of chapter 12 and the beginning of chapter 1, and the required adjustments would change the meaning of the story" (Schaarschmidt, 365–66).

Schaarschmidt succeeds in demonstrating that the placement of chapter 1 has a more than fortuitous importance for our appreciation of the story, and he makes a good case that Turner did not pursue the question of the first chapter far enough. On the other hand, it may be that Schaarschmidt has pursued it too far. His imaginative and linguistically complex analysis has located the function of chapter 1 within a pattern of organization that exists (granting that it does exist) at a very deep and not easily visible level of the text. He has, in fact, looked so deeply into the text that he seems to have neglected certain functions of chapter 1 that are more readily apparent. These are best seen in terms of the particular artistic problems Tolstoy faced in devising a chapter that, whatever other functions it may serve, is basically introductory in nature. We will examine the implications of chapter 1 considered as an introduction to the theme, the organizational structure of the chapter, and the system of images of the subsequent text. The goal is to provide another, more comprehensive, answer to Turner's excellent question: "Why is this chapter there?"

The title of the work clearly indicates two main factors: death and Ivan Ilich. Both make their first appearance in the story in a newspaper announcement, which brings the information to the attention of the public at large and to the particular notice of a group of Ivan Ilich's fellow judges during an interval in their work. Both the man and his death are in this way connected immediately to the motif of judgment. The "judicial" responsibility of rendering judgment of Ivan's death, suggested by the connection between the judges and the news, is, however, only partially carried out. In this respect it is significant that the desultory conversation of the judges prior to their becoming aware that Ivan Ilich has died concerns a question of "jurisdiction," but it is the finality of the announcement and the propriety of its conventional verbal formulas and customary sentiments that seem most effectively to absolve them from dealing with the essence of Ivan's death. The larger significance of the case of Ivan Ilich, it seems, is unappealably "closed" by the heavy black border of the funeral notice. The notice is written in the highly artificial and conventionalized language characteristic of such announcements. It is translated as follows: "Praskovya Fyodorovna Golovina, with profound sorrow, informs relatives and friends of the demise of her beloved husband Ivan Ilych Golovin, Member of the Court of Justice, which occurred on February the fourth of this year 1882" (123 [26:61]).

Ignoring the essential meaning of Ivan's demise, his colleagues concern themselves with its incidental concomitants: changes in official position and the like. Peter Ivanovich, however, feels obliged, as Ivan's oldest and closest friend, to pay a visit of condolence and respect to the bereaved. By attending the requiem and viewing the corpse Peter Ivanovich enters into a more immediate confrontation with death than was provided by the newspaper announcement. When he regards the severe countenance of his deceased associate, he comes "face to face" with death, the first example in this text of what I will describe as the metaphorization of experience, a topic about which I will say more in later chapters. The discomfort Peter Ivanovich experiences is ultimately neutralized, however, by his ability simply to walk away from the bier. Furthermore, death is, although more palpably present than before, still contained; on this occasion by the edge of the coffin, recalling the black border of the funeral announcement, and the chanting of the clerics, reminiscent of the stylized language of the printed notice. The saving grace of conventional conduct also helps to alleviate Peter Ivanovich's perplexity: "Peter Ivanovich . . . entered feeling uncertain what he would have to do. All he knew was that at such times it is always safe to cross oneself" (125 [26:63]).

Despite the various factors that shelter Peter Ivanovich from the reality of death, the dead face of Ivan Ilich produces a feeling of "disease" in him: "He felt a certain discomfort and so he hurriedly crossed himself once more, turned, and went out the door—too hurriedly and regardless of propriety, as he himself was aware" (125 [26:64]). The effect of Ivan Ilich's dead face is immediately counterbalanced by the gay and imperturbable countenance of Schwartz, an acquaintance of Peter Ivanovich who has also turned up for the memorial service: "The mere sight of that playful, well-groomed, and elegant figure restored Peter Ivanovich. He felt that Schwartz stood above all these happenings and would not surrender to any depressing influences" (126 [26:64]).

Peter Ivanovich's attitude at the requiem is ambivalent. He experiences discomfort followed by relief. These conflicting emotions are dramatically expressed by the juxtaposition of the images of Ivan Ilich and Schwartz. Ivan's face is sunken, solemn, and severe, and it gives the impression of being concerned with serious matters and the performance of inescapable responsibilities ("what was necessary had been accomplished" [125 (26:64)]); it is a reminder to the living of the reality of death and causes Peter Ivanovich's discomfort. Schwartz's face, on the contrary, is playful, and his concern is for that evening's game of cards; his "well-groomed" figure brims with life, and "the mere sight of him" is enough to restore Peter Ivanovich's habitual sense of contentment (126 [26:64]). These overt comparisons suggest one more: a contrast between darkness in Schwartz (his black garments, the significance of his name, which means "black" in German) and a presumed light in the dead Ivan.

Thus, an important thematic function of the first chapter is to provide an introductory account of the various attitudes toward the fact of Ivan's death. There is a gradual focusing apparent in the organization of this account, ranging from the breadth of the public at large and the opinions of Ivan's former colleagues, with their superficially polite but essentially callous indifference to his passing, through the similar attitude of Ivan's wife and family, the playful solemnity of Schwartz, and the severe countenance of the deceased himself. Each of these attitudes is reflected to the reader through Peter Ivanovich; ultimately, they are reduced to the competing sensations of discomfort and contentment he experiences.

As for the structural implications of the first chapter, it is evident that it provides a framework for the gradual reduction of attitudes toward Ivan's death from their general dimensions to the particular form they take within Peter Ivanovich. A second function is to provide the framework for a concurrent broadening of the image of Ivan Ilich himself, the other element of concern in the story's title. He is at first only a name in a frame (in the death notice), but he grows to become a face in a coffin and an object of discussion among those who knew him. To the face, then, is added an environment: his dead face communicates a "reproach and a warning to the living" (125 [26:64]). This second structural dimension is also conveyed through the medium of Peter Ivanovich. It is he who discovers the announcement in the newspaper, views the corpse, and is involved in all the reported conversations with Ivan's acquaintances and family. The two structural dimensions within the first chapter cooperate to produce a tension between what we see through Peter Ivanovich and what we see in him. The former is an ever-broadening view of Ivan Ilich from a printed name to a physical body to the human environment of which he was a part. The latter is an ever narrowing view of the impression created by Ivan's death from the universal joy that "it's he who is dead and not I" (124 [26:62]) to the calculating self-interest of his colleagues and family, to the personal obligations of his friends, and culminating in the ambivalence experienced by his closest friend, Peter Ivanovich.

On one hand the structure of the first chapter suggests that a continuing increase in the fullness and complexity of the representation of Ivan will follow, and it does. To the name and the face are added, in the course of the subsequent chapters, a past, a present, a mind, feelings, and ultimately a soul. On the other hand, chapter 1 offers a gradual focusing of the various attitudes toward death, which culminates in an unresolved question about the meaning of Ivan's demise. The two faces of Ivan and Schwartz, as mirrored in the perplexed mind of Peter Ivanovich, dramatically express the opposing sides in this implied debate. It is suggested that there is a need to choose between these mutually exclusive attitudes toward death, thus returning to the motif of death and judgment with which the chapter began. Since the particular death at issue is that of Ivan Ilich, it follows that the resolution of the question depends on the acquisition of further information about him, an acquisition that the gradual enlargement of Ivan's image in chapter 1 has also prepared us to expect.

Peter Ivanovich is central to both of the structural functions of the first chapter, but in the sequel he all but disappears. Perhaps this is merely the result of an abandoned structural plan (Peter Ivanovich was originally conceived as the narrator of the story). If so, it is remarkably fortuitous that his sudden disappearance leaves a gap of the right proportions to accommodate the reader who has, by seeing through the eyes and coming to know the mind of Peter Ivanovich, just been inspired with an unresolved affective tension in the face of death and the implicit desire to resolve it. It is perhaps not simply coincidence that Peter Ivanovich was first presented as a reader (of the newspaper). It is, at least, certain to be the reader of the story who will, from chapter 2 on, observe the increasingly full delineation of Ivan Ilich, and it is also the reader who will continue Peter Ivanovich's abandoned internal struggle to find the proper attitude toward death. The profound irony of the narrator's tone in chapter 1 makes at least one thing absolutely clear: Peter Ivanovich's ultimate disregard of his internal dilemma is not a satisfactory solution of it.

A characteristic feature of the further development of the portrait of Ivan Ilich, on the basis of which the reader is invited to render judgment, is the frequent recurrence of episodes, details, and metaphors closely associated with the motif of enclosure and delimitation suggested in chapter 1 by the references to the black border of the death notice and the edge of Ivan's coffin. The importance of these two original images of confinement for the text as a whole can scarcely be overestimated, for chapters 2 through 12 contain an entire network of references that seem to arise from them.

We are told that although Ivan, as a young man, was more unpredictable than his stodgy elder brother, his behavior always remained "within limits which his instinct unfailingly indicated to him as correct" (130 [26:70]). We learn that the quality that, above all others, enabled him to succeed in his work was his capacity to reduce even the most complex matters to the confines of a correctly drawn document. This ability derives from his mastery of the "method of eliminating all considerations irrelevant to the legal aspect of the case" (132 [26:72]). He applies this method with equal severity to the nagging complexities of his married life, once it becomes clear to him that a "definite" attitude (the Russian word, translated as "definite," also means "delimited" [134 (26:74)]) is as needful at home as at work.

Not surprisingly, the judicial *isolation* that he strives for and that becomes characteristic of his official position is mirrored by domestic *alienation*.

The effect of the network of barriers that Ivan had gradually erected around himself is exacerbated by the onset and progress of his illness. As his sufferings increase he withdraws more and more from the life of those around him. He ceases to participate in his favorite amusements and is portrayed as overhearing others at play from "behind the door" of an adjacent room. He confines himself more and more to his study until he seems permanently installed there, lying upon the sofa with his face turned to the back. As his sufferings increase, Ivan seeks to protect himself from them. When his resolve simply to ignore his pain proved unworkable, he sought "other screens" behind which to take shelter. He realizes that he has become a "constraint" on the freedom of others and that they have begun to block him out of their lives. Eventually, he experiences a "loneliness [or isolation] . . . that could not have been more complete anywhere— either at the bottom of the sea or under the earth" (162 [26:108]).

All of these examples, and their number could easily be multiplied, are reflections of the original images of confinement, constraint, and enclosure presented in chapter 1. The later examples grow, as from a seed, from the black border of the death notice and the framing effect of Ivan's coffin. Yet, at the same time, these original images are paradoxically also the final strands in the intertwining web of metaphor and incident that the story contains. The text, in this sense, turns out to be an account of how it happened that Ivan Ilich changed from a normal, ordinary, living man into something that could be conveniently fitted into the tiny frame of a funeral notice.

The problem of chapter 1 is to be solved, therefore, by regarding it as an introduction that, besides affording an opportunity for the traditional presentation of the central characters and situation, is rich in implications for the theme, structure, and dominant images of the subsequent text. Thematically, it establishes the contrasting postures of decorous indifference and spiritual unease as irreducible polarities in an implied debate about the appropriate attitude to the protagonist's death. Structurally, it creates an expectation of the more complete portrait of Ivan and his life, which is supplied in chapters 2 through 12. In accomplishing this, it incorporates one of the story's central images: that of the enclosing or bordering effect of the black frame of Ivan's death notice and the edge of his coffin. These early expressions of the forces that confine and crush the protagonist are extensively developed in chapters 2 through 12 and are ultimately reincarnated in the image of the black bag in chapter 9 and echoed again in chapter 12 when "what had been oppressing him and would not leave him was all dropping away at once, *from two sides, from ten sides, from all sides*" (167 [26:113]; emphasis mine). Finally, it may be suggested that chapter 1 performs the hortatory function of inviting the reader to assume the role of observer and judge so conveniently abandoned at the end of the chapter by Peter Ivanovich's hasty departure for an evening of cards. Thus, the reader is subtly instructed as to the approach to be adopted toward what follows; deciding the significance of the death of Ivan Ilich has become the duty of the reader.

6

Life

In this chapter we will consider chapters 2 through 4 in which information about Ivan Ilich's life up to and including the onset of his illness is presented. I will be interested in drawing attention to situations and images associated with Ivan's life before his illness that will later resonate with those in which his illness develops (chapters 5 through 8) and in which he dies (chapter 9 through 12).

CHAPTER 2

In order to arrive at a judgment as to the significance of the death of Ivan Ilich—a task that, as we saw in the preceding chapter, was implicitly entrusted to us—we, as readers, will need to have data on both Ivan's death and the manner of his life. Chapter 2 provides information about the early years of the protagonist's life.

The chapter begins with one of Tolstoy's most often quoted lines: "Ivan Ilych's life had been most simple and most ordinary, and most terrible" (129 [26:68]). We learn that Ivan Ilich dies at the age of 45. By putting together the information presented in chapter 2 (and here and there in the other chapters) the editors of the standard scholarly text of *The Death of Ivan Ilich* have compiled the following rough chronology of the life of the protagonist (26:686). I offer it here as a convenient overview of the most obvious level of the novel's content.

1837—The birth, in St. Petersburg, of Ivan Ilich Golovin in the family of Privy Councillor Ilya Efimovich Golovin

1850s—Ivan Ilich's education in the School of Law.

1859—Ivan Ilich's graduation from the School of Law.

1859–1864—First years of government service as an apprentice official entrusted with various duties.

1864—Ivan Ilich adapts very well to the changes wrought in the legal system by the wide-ranging judicial reforms of the early 1860s. Transfer and promotion to court investigator.

1866—Marriage to Praskovya Fyodorovna Mikhel.

1867—Birth of daughter, Liza.

1867—Ivan Ilich's promotion to prosecutor.

1869—Birth of son, Vasily.

1871—Ivan Ilich transferred to a third province.

1878—Son, Vasily, begins studies at a private school.

1879—Ivan Ilich bypassed for promotion; he quarrels with Hoppe, who received the promotion, and with his immediate superiors.

1880—Having fallen into disfavor with his superiors, Ivan Ilich is once again bypassed for promotion. He spends the summer with his wife's brother at the latter's home in the country. He goes to St. Petersburg to find a position in a different government department. Changes in the top administration of the Ministry of Justice bring an unexpected reversal of Ivan Ilich's recent misfortunes. He is promoted and transferred from the provinces to one of the major cities (the drafts of the novel specify Moscow, but this detail does not appear in the final published text).

Autumn 1880—Ivan Ilich begins his new appointment. While decorating his new apartment he falls from a stepladder and bumps his side.

Autumn 1881—The onset of Ivan Ilich's disease. Consultations with various doctors.

January 1882—Ivan Ilich's condition takes a turn for the worse. Insomnia, pain, the use of drugs. Consultation with a famous doctor.

Late January 1882—Daughter, Liza, is engaged to Fyodor Petrovich Petrishchev, a court investigator. Ivan Ilich's condition takes a sharp turn for the worse.

1 February 1882—Ivan Ilich's final agony begins.

4 February 1882—The death of Ivan Ilich.

As the first sentence of chapter 2 suggests, the main point of Ivan's life is the fact that it is so ordinary and unremarkable. We learn that he was the middle of three sons, both in age and in character: neither as stodgy as his elder brother nor as wild as the younger. "He was a happy mean between them" (130 [26:69]), suggesting also the "average" and the "golden mean." Indeed, he will live his life as though consciously striving to realize the classical ideal of "nothing too much" (one of two mottoes inscribed on the walls of the Temple of Apollo at Delphi). The later references (in chapter 6) to Kiesewetter's book on logic, which was an actual textbook of syllogistic logic, remind us of this classical motif, as does the Latin motto inscribed on Ivan's watch. The unspoken suggestion would seem to be that we, as readers, ought not, as Ivan seems to do, to forget the second of the two Delphic ideals: "know thyself."

Ivan's youth is guided by a "sense" that he has for not overstepping the bounds of permissible behavior; he always seems to know the extent to which the indulgence of those highly placed in society (to whom he is attracted as "a moth to flame," an action fatal to the moth) can be tested. He remains always within "known limits" (130 [26:70]). His career in the legal institute is unremarkable, and he concludes it with a series of conventional purchases (clothing and luggage; a charm, engraved with a traditional lawyer's motto, "respice finem" ["look to the end," "take the long view"], for his watch chain; a traditional celebratory dinner at a fashionable restaurant) and sets off for his first posting, as an "official on special instructions" (i.e., a glorified "gofer") for a provincial governor.

His sense of fitness, already noted, continues to serve him well. As his responsibilities increase, so does the gravity of his deportment. He senses the changes overtaking the judiciary (among the major reforms that followed the liberation of the serfs in 1861 were judicial reforms) and takes advantage of them by adapting himself to new requirements, by "becoming the new man" that the new institutions of justice required (132 [26:71]). He is unfailingly attentive to the good opinion of those of higher social position than himself. His marriage to Praskovya Fyodorovna is motivated in part by his sense that "it was considered the right thing to do by the most highly placed of his associates" (133 [26:73]).

Ivan Ilich at first finds his married life to be pleasant and uncomplicated, but this idyll of domestic bliss is soon shattered by his wife's first pregnancy and the change in her behavior this produces. An important passage provides a list of the major characteristics of Ivan Ilich's life: "easy, agreeable, pleasant, and always decorous . . . approved of by society" (133 [26:73]). His pregnant wife's behavior, however, seems to him to threaten all that he holds most dear. She becomes jealous of him, demands excessive attention, is irritable, and makes unpleasant scenes. In short, she behaves very much in the manner later characteristic of Ivan as his illness progresses, which suggests that these symptoms are characteristic of the imminence of new life.

Ivan responds to these changes in his life by increasing his isolation from the source of his discomfort. He discovers that his work is the only "excuse" accepted by Praskovya Fyodorovna for his failure to fall in with her moods or wishes; consequently, his life's center of gravity moves more and more into the official sphere of his professional judicial activities. "He only required of [his family life] those conveniences—dinner at home, housewife, and bed—which it could give him, and above all that propriety of external forms required by public opinion. For the rest, he looked for light-hearted pleasure and propriety, and was very thankful when he found them, but if he met with antagonism and querulousness he retired at once into his separate, fenced-off world of official duties, where he found satisfaction" (134 [26:74–75]). In this way, Tolstoy establishes that (1) Ivan's idea of the quality of a life is measured by its agreement with the strictly delimited and highly conventionalized ideal promoted by the opinion of society; (2) that such a life is possible until it is disrupted by the advent of a new life; (3) that Ivan's response to the loss of his conventionalized ideal is to isolate himself as much as possible from the destructive influences. We might read this as suggesting that Ivan's old life is threatened by the arrival of new life and that his response to this threat is to retreat from the new life ever more into the old life. We wonder, is one of these "lives" not really life at all?

Ivan Ilich is a model official. He has a great talent for isolating himself as a human being from the cases that come before him and dealing with them in a strictly judicial or official manner. Thus, he is skilled in formulating even the most complicated matters on paper in the proper way and excluding every vestige of his personal views (132 [26:72]). He succeeds at work. He never exceeds his authority, and he works diligently to fulfill all the requirements of his duties. His career continues to make slow, steady progress all the while his children are growing up.

CHAPTER 3

Seventeen years have elapsed between the beginning of this chapter and the end of the preceding one. Tolstoy's strategy in the presentation of Ivan Ilich's life is now clear; he means to present descriptions of a series of biographical moments. In chapter 2 he presented Ivan Ilich as a young man, just out of law school, and followed him through his first steps up the ladder of official success. Then Tolstoy skipped ahead to the period of Ivan Ilich's marriage and his first year of married life. Now another, this time rather lengthy, period has elapsed. Ivan has reached a position of solid success; he now turns down transfers to new positions, awaiting one he will consider most desirable (135 [26:76]). The smooth course of his life is, however, interrupted at this point by an "unpleasant occurrence [which] quite upset the peaceful course of his life" (135 [26:76]). He is bypassed for promotion, takes offense at this and complains (angering his superiors), and is bypassed again.

The attentive reader will note that this is not the first time that the calm proceeding of Ivan's life has been interrupted. We know already of two prior occasions where roughly the same thing happened. When Ivan was in law school "he had done things which had formerly [i.e., when he was a child] seemed to him very horrid and made him feel disgusted with himself when he did them; but later on when he saw that such actions were done by people of good position and that they did not regard them as wrong, he was not exactly able to regard them as right, but to forget about them entirely or not be troubled at all by remembering them" (130 [26:70]). Again, when his wife became pregnant, he sensed that something was wrong with his life; we saw that he addressed this problem by withdrawing ever more into his official duties. In effect, his problem in both of these instances is the sensation that something is wrong, not as it should be in his life, and his solution is to ignore the problem, either by forgetting about it or by withdrawing from it.

Now, at the beginning of chapter 3, his life is once again upset; again, the problem involves what seems to Ivan to be a disruption of the proper order of things. On this occasion, however, the problem is not personal or familial, but besets him at work. It would seem that unpleasantness has followed Ivan Ilich into his official refuge. There is no place to which he can flee from this trouble; consequently, he attempts to confront it directly. His complaints, however, only make the matter worse. In the end, filled with a sense of righteous anger at the injustices done to him, he decides to seek a new position. A pattern seems to be emerging here: a moment in Ivan's life is described; its normal flow is disturbed by some sensation or event; Ivan attempts to deal with the disruption by withdrawing from its source. Here again the "normal" flow of life is restored, but this time in a different way. A sudden change in the highest administration of the Ministry of Justice results in a close friend of Ivan's coming into great authority. This introduces a new note into the theme Tolstoy has been playing on Ivan's life: normalcy (that is, a pleasant life) is restored not by Ivan's efforts, but by chance. This turn of events has certain implications that will be of importance later in novel. One implication is that Ivan is in error about the nature of his official life. He has become used to thinking of it as a safe refuge from unpleasantness, as a part of his life that runs predictably and that remains under his control. We might note that from this point of view, Ivan's official life resembles the card games of which he is so fond: conducted within clear, simple, and consistent rules and accompanied by a set of reasonable conventions designed to ensure the preservation of harmony and propriety. It now happens, however, that the promotion that should have gone to Ivan (because he has fulfilled all of his obligations toward the service) is denied him; the promotion is given to another, not on the basis of order and predictability, but unexpectedly, almost randomly. Even more alarming, when he uses the mechanisms of complaint officially established to redress such injustice, matters become still worse. Ivan's official life is not operating as he imagines it ought to. Worst of all, Ivan's restoration in the Ministry and his promotion are the result of still another incursion of chance and randomness into the official world, the unexpected and sudden promotion of his friend. Ivan, of course, is so relieved by the fortunate *result* of this new incursion of the unpredictable into his life that he is able to overlook the fact that it was unpredictable. He is left with the comfortable illusion that his life is solid and predictable, as it had been before, even though the events described show clearly that it is not. The reader, however, should note that Ivan Ilich's official life depends upon illusion and that his contentment depends upon his ability to ignore the obvious significance of what has occurred. As a matter of fact, the true position is suggested by a line from the text. In describing Ivan's preparations to undertake his new position Tolstoy notes that Ivan felt the need for time to "set himself up": "in a word, to make arrangements as he had resolved on [in his mind]" (137 [26:78]). Ivan believes that he has the power to control his life, to make it take the shape he wants it to have, despite the fact that events have proven that he has no such power.

Ivan Ilich undertakes the establishment of himself and his family in the major city to which his new appointment sends him. Leaving his wife and family in the country, he travels to the city, finds a "charming" apartment, "just the thing both he and his wife had dreamt about" (137 [26:78]), and sets himself to the task of supervising its furnishing and decoration. His every effort is crowned with unexceptionable success in achieving a style *comme il faut* (French for "in the best taste," "in accord with the most current fashion"). As we learn from the text "everything progressed and approached the ideal he had set himself" (137 [26:78–79]).

In the course of these preparations Ivan falls from a stepladder while demonstrating to a workman how he wants the draperies hung. He strikes his side against a protruding handle; there is pain, but it soon passes. Ivan continues to feel both "happy and healthy" (138 [26:79]). As it turns out, however, this apparently unremarkable event, described in two sentences, will represent the beginning of a crisis in Ivan Ilich's life. With the benefit of hindsight it may well seem significant that Ivan Ilich falls from a ladder just at the point when, in his career, he has finally reached the upper rungs on the ladder of success. Again, that he falls while adjusting a drapery resonates significantly with the insistent use of images of borders, curtains, and boundaries to suggest Ivan Ilich's growing and voluntary isolation noted in our discussion of chapter 1. (We cannot fail to observe that he has decided to decorate his apartment alone.) Finally, his fall is the apparent physical cause of the illness that eventually kills him, and his death is thus obliquely linked to his official career and to his habit of isolating himself. In short, Ivan's career and his concern with the establishment of an ideal manner of life conforming to society's view of good taste, which are for him the very center and essence of his life, are suggested in this incident of the fall to be more appropriately associated with his death. The attentive reader will also not miss the Judeo-Christian religious implications of Ivan's "falling" at the moment in which he feels that his ideal has been reached (as Adam falls from grace in the Garden of Eden); the same sort of significance may attach to the fact that Ivan is struck in the side as he falls, suggesting a comparison with the wound received by Christ on the cross. This matter will be touched upon again in chapter 8 of this book.

The remainder of chapter 3 attaches growing importance to the fall by referring to it once more. Following the triumphant tour of the newly decorated apartment on which Ivan Ilich conducts his wife and children after their arrival in the city, Praskovya Fyodorovna inquires about his injury. Ivan Ilich responds in a light vein, explaining that it is a good thing he keeps himself in top physical condition because "another man might have been killed" (138 [26:80]). In general, however, the remainder of this chapter is devoted to a lengthy description of the manner of Ivan Ilich's life once his transfer to his new appointment is complete. His life consists of three separate divisions. His official life is conducted in the familiar manner of "knowing how to exclude everything fresh and vital" from his relations with those who come before him in his work, because to do otherwise would be to "disturb the regular course of official business" (139 [26:80]). His social life consists of pleasant, formal contacts between himself and guests drawn from the ranks of the "best society" (140 [26:82]); these contacts are described in the Russian original as "time spending" and are mainly remarkable for the fact that they are in no way different from any of the other "time spendings" of the people involved. These social occasions are as alike one to another as are the parlors in the homes in which they take place (140 [26:81]). Best of all to Ivan Ilich is his bridge-playing life. "But Ivan Ilych's greatest pleasure was playing bridge. He acknowledged that . . . the pleasure that beamed like a ray of sunshine above everything else was to sit down to bridge with good players, not noisy partners, . . . to play a clever and serious game" (140 [26:82]).

Ivan Ilich's life is remarkable for its stability and orderliness, its consistency and predictability. The examples given in the last couple of pages of chapter 3 suggest that these qualities are the result of the expulsion of all of the messy and unpredictable qualities of human life and their replacement with a facsimile of friendly human relationships, which, as at work, so at home, Ivan Ilich felt capable of throwing off at any time if they became a hindrance to the easy, pleasant, and proper flow of life. As readers, we now see that Ivan Ilich's fascination with cards, which had been mentioned earlier but is described in detail in chapter 3, is the result of the powerful analogy between the conduct of a well-played game of bridge and the sort of life that he imagines as ideal. At the end of chapter 3, Ivan Ilich has in fact attained this ideal form of life; he has successfully ignored every warning life has sent him over the years, including the randomly produced basis of his current success, in order to believe in the solidity of the life he believes he has created for himself. However, just as his lovingly chosen and arranged furniture shows an occasional irritating blemish ("every spot on a tablecloth ... was painful to him," 141 [26:80]), so, too, he himself, his own real flesh, now carries a spot, the bruise that remains on his side after his fall and the pain of which, although less, is still not completely past (141 [26:80]).

CHAPTER 4

This chapter describes the onset of Ivan Ilich's ultimately fatal illness. The text of the preceding chapter had referred several times to the incident of Ivan Ilich's fall and the resulting persistent bruise and slight discomfort. These signs now manifest themselves ever more seriously. The first few paragraphs of the chapter describe the onset of the first symptoms: a feeling of clumsiness, a strange taste in the mouth, fits of irritability and anger, a propensity to disrupt the easy, pleasant, and proper flow of life. It is worth noting that these symptoms match the symptoms and behavior ascribed to Praskovya Fyodorovna during her pregnancy (described in chapter 2 [133 (26:74)]). Odd as it may seem, then, the onset of Ivan Ilich's illness, which will lead to his death, is characterized by the same symptoms as Praskovya Fyodorovna's pregnancy, which culminates in the arrival of new life. This is the first of many such hints to the effect that Ivan Ilich's death is associated with his discovery of a new meaning of life; conversely, of course, the suggestion is that Ivan Ilich's present life is actually a form of death. Also of note in this passage is that Praskovya Fyodorovna reacts to Ivan Ilich's lapses from accepted behavior in much the same way as he formerly reacted to her. She tries to minimize contact with him and to speed through whatever contacts may be required. Unlike Ivan, who had been able to take refuge in the world of his work, she has nowhere she can go in order to escape dealing with him. She secretly desires his death (141 [26:83]), but this would be no solution since if he dies, his salary will of course cease as well.

In due course Ivan Ilich decides to consult a specialist. As Praskovya Fyodorovna, mutatis mutandis, treats him as he had treated her, so now the specialist (and all the other doctors whom Ivan Ilich will

consult) treats him as he had always treated the petitioners who came
before him in court. In the doctor's office "it was all as it was in the
law courts" (142 [26:84]). Ivan Ilich is mainly concerned to know
whether his condition is dangerous—that is, he wants to know the
personal, individual significance of his illness; the doctors are concerned rather with such questions as whether Ivan Ilich is suffering
from "a floating kidney, a chronic catarrh, or appendicitis" (142
[26:84])—that is, with purely medical questions. At this point the
reader must recall the passage in chapter 2 that described Ivan Ilich's
special fitness for his legal duties: his ability to distance himself from
any circumstances that had nothing to do, strictly speaking, with the
service and to treat even the most complex matter in a manner that
deprived it of all of its personal significance and retained only its purely
formal aspects (132 [26:72]). This passage even contains a pun that
draws our attention to the similarity between the doctors' treating
(*lechenie*) of Ivan's illness and his own manner of treating (*oblechenie*)
complex legal questions as though they were devoid of personal significance. Finally, as he leaves, the doctor looks at Ivan Ilich as though
to say: "Prisoner, if you will not keep to the questions put to you, I
shall be obliged to have you removed from the court" (142 [26:84]).

In describing the efforts of the doctors Tolstoy becomes quite
ironic, a propensity we can observe throughout his works. The scene
in *Anna Karenina* (at the beginning of part 2) in which Kitty is examined by a doctor is a case in point. Despite Tolstoy's rather obvious
disdain for doctors, there has been some scholarly investigation of the
question of exactly what Ivan Ilich was suffering from (see chapter 3
of this book). It is important to note that the doctors (and, of course,
Ivan Ilich in his legal career) address themselves to a question that is
of peripheral rather than central concern. Since they confine themselves
to Ivan Ilich's bodily ills, we may well conclude that it is the spiritual
dimension of Ivan Ilich's life that most urgently requires attention.

Ivan Ilich attempts to follow the doctor's advice exactly, which
means that he attempts to treat his illness as though it were of purely
physiological concern. "From the time of his visit to the doctor, Ivan
Ilych's chief occupation was the exact fulfillment of his doctor's instructions regarding hygiene and the taking of medicine, and the observation of his pain and his excretions" (143 [26:85]). Thus, he, too,

tries to adopt the position that his illness is of purely physiological concern. Chapters 5 through 8 describe the gradual break down of Ivan Ilich's reluctance to admit that he is much more seriously sick in the spiritual sense than he is in the physiological one.

Ivan Ilich's efforts to follow doctor's orders are symptomatic of his belief that life is, or should be, pleasant and well regulated. When confronted with a phenomenon that disrupts this image of life, Ivan's reaction has been to ignore the disruption, or attempt to deal with it through the proper channels, or to remove himself from the sphere of its effect. As he dealt with his wife's disruptive behavior when she was pregnant and with his being passed over for promotion,[1] so, too, with his illness, he first tries to take the appropriate steps to correct his condition, as though his illness were an anticipated disruption of the pleasant flow of life and could be corrected by the application of well-known measures. At the same time, we learn that he also tries to ignore the effects of his disease: "The pain did not diminish [from following doctor's orders], but Ivan Ilich made efforts to force himself to think that he was better. He could do this so long as nothing agitated him" (143 [26:86]). At this point, the theme of self-deception, which has already been suggested by his unacknowledged understanding of what caused his promotion, now becomes overt in the text. It will lead eventually to the question of whether Ivan Ilich's life has been increasingly based on self-deception and ultimately whether his very understanding of life is not a form of self-deception.

The pain of Ivan Ilich's illness increases when he is upset by the behavior of his wife, or by a mishap at work, or by bad cards at bridge (143 [26:86]). This would seem to suggest that these things cause the pain that he experiences; how can that be? One explanation would be that all of the examples mentioned represent violations of Ivan Ilich's understanding of the proper course and experience of life. We are then relying on our previously stated analysis of the game of bridge as a metaphor for Ivan's ideal of a life well lived. All of these items, then, would be of the sort to cause Ivan Ilich to experience discomfort or pain. He has found ways of dealing, by deceiving himself, with the pain of the first three; he will find that it is impossible to deal with the pain of his illness. In the end he will be forced to deal with his pain by recognizing its significance rather than by finding a way to neutralize it or escape from it. Pursuing the topic a little further, it may be appropriate to speculate that if Ivan Ilich's understanding of life is the worse of his two "sicknesses" then the moral pain he experiences may, as with a physical illness, be a signal of dysfunction and be better treated by removing the cause of the pain rather than by alleviating the symptoms. In this case Ivan Ilich's consultations with other celebrated doctors would represent an attempt to deal with the painful symptoms—his physical illness—rather than with the underlying spiritual dysfunction the physical illness seems to represent.

In any case, his visits to various doctors, and various kinds of doctors, do not provide any relief. He even briefly considers making a pilgrimage to try the efficacy of wonder-working icons as a cure for his illness. This resonates interestingly with the episode of the sudden reversal of his declining fortunes in his work in chapter 3. There, too, his effort to deal with his problem (being twice passed over for promotion) through the proper channels is unsuccessful; his reinstatement in official favor and the aggrandizement of his position is the result of what might well be called a "miracle"—the completely unexpected change in the hierarchy of the Ministry. None of his efforts to deal with his illness as a physical problem is of any help, however. "The pain in his side oppressed him and seemed to grow worse and more incessant, while the taste in his mouth grew stranger and stranger. It seemed to him that his breath had a disgusting smell, and he was conscious of a loss of appetite and strength. There was no deceiving himself; something terrible, new, and more important than anything before in his life, was taking place within him of which he alone was aware" (144 [26:87]). Once again, the suggestion is that the physical illness is a sign of something beyond itself, something not treatable by doctors.

Praskovya Fyodorovna's insistence on the idea that the reason Ivan Ilich fails to get better is his inability (or refusal) to follow doctor's orders conscientiously is indicative of Ivan Ilich's growing isolation from those around him. He experiences the same sense of isolation at work. It is as though his illness has become the central feature of his identity. His colleagues vacillate between speculation as to the filling of Ivan Ilich's place in the service, as soon as his illness should force him to leave it, and an attitude of playfulness and jest, which suggests a refusal to take Ivan Ilich's condition seriously. Ivan Ilich is particularly irritated by Schwarz's "playfulness, liveliness, and *comme il faut* demeanor," which remind him, above all, of himself 10 years younger (145 [26:88]). This provides an interesting echo of the effect of these qualities of Schwarz on Peter Ivanovich in chapter 1. There Schwarz's playful, lively, smiling demeanor dispels the feelings of anxiety occasioned in Peter Ivanovich by his confrontation with the dead face of Ivan Ilich. Finally, even Ivan Ilich's enjoyment of bridge is spoiled by the constant, sucking pain. Even with a good hand to play "it seemed to him that there was something wild in his being able to rejoice in the possibility of slam" when he felt so ill; even worse, he becomes so irritated with his feelings that he misplays the hand and goes down three. Ivan Ilich's home life, his work life, and the card game that symbolizes the ideal of life as he conceives it are all devastated, made null, by the unceasing pain his illness brings.

At the end of chapter 4 Ivan Ilich's illness has become the central fact of his life, has ruined every aspect of the life he has so patiently constructed over the years, and, far from abating, shows every sign of becoming worse. In our discussion of chapter 1 it was suggested that the function of the remaining chapters was to provide information that would allow us to understand how it was that Ivan Ilich had been reduced to the point of being no more than a name in the conventional frame of a funeral notice. Chapter 2 through 4 have provided this information for the greater part of Ivan Ilich's life; at the end of chapter 4 Ivan Ilich has barely two months left to live. Tolstoy has throughout these chapters been at pains to emphasize the irony of Ivan Ilich's position. It has been shown that Ivan Ilich's method of dealing with life's unpleasantnesses has always been to avoid them or close himself off from them, if he wasn't able to correct them. By the end of chapter 4 Ivan Ilich himself has become "an unpleasantness," and all those around him are beginning to cut themselves off from him, to isolate him (and his pain) from themselves. At the same time, it has become clear that there is an intimate linkage among various episodes in Ivan Ilich's life: the "shameful" acts of his youth (which shame he soon forgot when he understood that all the other boys were doing the same); the unpleasantness caused by the unseemly behavior of the pregnant Praskovya Fyodorovna; the injustice of being passed over for promotion; and finally the pain, indignity, and growing isolation caused by his illness. I have suggested that each of these, not only the last, functions in the novel as a message to Ivan Ilich that the way in which he understands life is defective. In each case, except the last (the case of his illness), he has managed to ignore, or chance has allowed him to escape from, the import of these messages. His illness and its pain, however, prove to be inescapable. The next four chapters of the novel (chapters 5 through 8) represent Ivan Ilich's struggle to come to terms with the illness he cannot escape, the message he cannot ignore. We turn to consideration of these chapters in the next section of this book.

7

Illness

The first four chapters of *The Death of Ivan Ilich*, as we have seen, have provided an account of Ivan Ilich's life from his childhood through the onset of his illness at the age of about 45. The second set of four chapters, chapter 5 through chapter 8, covers a much shorter period of time—a span of only about two months. As I mentioned earlier (in chapter 4), the lengths of these chapters reflect the fact that they are concerned with a much more compressed period of time; these chapters average only half the length of the first four chapters. This suggests that time is growing shorter for Ivan Ilich as his illness progresses from incipient to terminal.

In these chapters Ivan Ilich suffers catastrophic physiological deterioration. He gradually becomes aware that his illness will not respond to the standard methods of treatment. He is driven more and more to contemplate and understand the significance of his situation.

CHAPTER 5

This chapter begins with the arrival of Ivan Ilich's brother-in-law for a New Year's visit. The look of astonishment and dismay on his visitor's face tells Ivan Ilich most plainly that his illness has wrought a dreadful change in him. He sees for himself, by comparing his image in the mirror with a photograph of himself, that he has suffered a dreadful physical decline. He eavesdrops on the private conversation of Praskovya Fyodorovna and her brother and learns that the visitor thinks that "Ivan Ilich is a dead man" (147 [26:89]).

Ivan Ilich resolves to visit yet one more doctor. This doctor diagnoses a dysfunction of the caecum and prescribes medication he says will restore the balance of the organs and lead to a cure. Ivan Ilich is much relieved by what the doctor tells him; he passes the rest of the day in his former fashion—working on legal papers, visiting with guests. After retiring for the night he begins to imagine the dysfunction of the caecum and the gradual restoration of balance in his organs as the new doctor's therapy begins to produce its intended results. Ivan Ilich feels much better, he can almost see in imagination the proper functioning of the appendix being restored. Immediately, however, "he felt the old, familiar, dull, gnawing pain, stubborn and serious" (148 [26:91]).

The return of his pain marks a turning point in the progress of Ivan Ilich's disease. He becomes discouraged with the advice of doctors and with the very idea that doctors can help him. Suddenly he sees his situation from a new and different point of view. " 'Vermiform appendix! Kidney!' he said to himself. 'It's not a question of my appendix or my kidney, but of life and . . . death. Yes, life was there and now it's going, going and I cannot stop it. Yes. Why deceive myself?' " (148 [26:91]). Here Ivan Ilich takes the first steps toward grappling with his illness as other than a purely medical problem. For the first time, he conceives of his situation as one in which he finds himself caught not between health and sickness but between life and death.

For the first time the appalling thought of death becomes fully real for Ivan Ilich. Tolstoy sprinkles the text with such significant phrases as "tried to light a candle," "turned cold," "his breathing stopped," "stared with open eyes into the darkness" (148–49 [26:91]). In the context, all of these can be understood as ordinary and even trivial actions: what more normal than to light a candle if the room is dark, or to shiver, or to catch one's breath, or (having dropped the candle on the floor) to sit in the dark? At the same time, they point clearly to Ivan Ilich's dawning realization of his own mortality. He realizes, too, that he is not alone, that everyone is condemned to death. The reader can hardly fail to notice at this point that a marked change in the narrative strategy has taken place. The situation of Ivan Ilich, which had until now been described from the outside by the narrator of the story, now begins to be shown by reporting the contents of his own mental reflections. The narrator continues to direct and organize the narrative, but from this point on the role played by reports of Ivan Ilich's mental state grows steadily in importance. This suggests that this middle set of chapters is concerned not only with the external, perhaps superficial, dimensions of Ivan Ilich's life, but now also with his internal states. As readers who remember that the task delivered to us at the end of chapter 1 (to judge the significance of Ivan Ilich's death) is still before us, we will be especially interested in the view of things as seen from within. Until now, we have been mainly in the same position as the doctors with whom Ivan Ilich consulted. We were allowed to view the case from the outside; we were shown the sickness rather than the person who was sick. Now that will begin to change. To follow up the metaphor suggested by the story itself, we will begin to look at the case of Ivan Ilich with all the individualizing details left in rather than "reduced to the proper form on a single sheet of paper." Ivan Ilich's first horrified and painfully vivid glimpse of death's reality is followed immediately by doubts of the verity of his perception. He thinks over the entire course of his illness yet again, but the result is the same. He arrives at death and terror, again tries and fails to light a candle, again collapses helplessly onto the sofa (148 [26:92]).

CHAPTER 6

In chapter 5 Ivan Ilich becomes convinced that he is more than simply ill; he is in fact dying. To know that he is dying and to understand it, however, prove to be different things. Logic is no help. The effect of logic is to remove everything individual from cases, to treat all individuals precisely as instances of generalities. Thus, Ivan Ilich finds no understanding in the exemplary syllogism from Kiesewetter's textbook of logic, remembered from his years in school: "Caius is a man, all men are mortal, therefore, Caius is mortal." "Caius really was mortal, and it was right for him to die; but as for me, little Vanya, Ivan Ilich, with all my thoughts and emotions, it's altogether a different matter. It cannot be that I ought to die. That would be too terrible" (150 [26:93]).

He tries again and again to "get back into the former current of thought" (150 [26:93]) that had concealed death from him. Whatever he does and wherever he is, however, his pain returns and begins again its steady, gnawing work. Making use of the fact that in Russian both "pain" (bol') and "death" (smert') are feminine nouns—and, consequently, replaceable by the pronoun ona which could be translated into English as either "she" or "it")—Tolstoy deliberately confuses the two in Ivan Ilich's reflections on his situation. Just as there is no refuge from the pain, so there is also no refuge from death. Try as he will, Ivan Ilich is incapable of avoiding, ignoring, escaping from death. Pain/death besets him at work and at home, while concerned with official business or with domestic arrangements, in company and alone. Tolstoy refers to his attempts to escape this constant awareness of death as "new screens," which "for a while seemed to save him, but then they immediately fell to pieces or rather became transparent, as if It [Pain/death] penetrated them and nothing could veil It" (151 [26:94]). In the end there comes a moment when he sees It looking at him from behind the flowers in the parlor, the room for which, as he thinks, "he sacrificed his life" (151 [26:94]) and later "he lost his life" (151 [26:95]). His life is over: "Is that possible? How terrible and how stupid! It can't be true! It can't, but it is" (151 [26:95]). At the end of chapter 6 Ivan Ilich is "face to face with death, and there is nothing to be done about it. The only thing there is to do is to look at it, and to grow cold" (26:95).

The last phrase of chapter 6 is often translated as "to shudder" (as in the Maude translation [151]). Indeed, that is what happens when one feels cold. As with so many phrases in the novel, however, the reader needs to pay attention to the figurative meaning of direct usages (e.g., Ivan Ilich's "staring into the darkness" or "trying to light a candle" in chapter 5) and the direct meaning of figurative usages (Peter Ivanovich coming "face to face" with death while viewing the corpse of his departed friend in chapter 1). So here, "to grow cold" metonymically suggests "to shudder," and consequently "to shudder" is a defensible translation. But the Russian word also speaks directly to a fall in the temperature of its subject. Since that subject (Ivan Ilich) is face to face with death, the phrase suggests that death has overtaken him.

And yet, Ivan Ilich is clearly not yet dead. He will die only at the very end of the novel, in chapter 12. What is the significance of the insistence in chapter 5 and chapter 6 that he is *already* dead or as good as dead? One of the implications of encountering the death of Ivan Ilich at the end of chapter 6 would be that the hypothesis of a three-part organization of the text (as suggested by our consideration of chapter lengths and contents in chapter 4) may need to be revised to accommodate the presence of so significant an event at the mid-point of this 12-chapter novel. The implied death of Ivan Ilich at the end of chapter 6, especially when paired with his apparent rebirth at the end of chapter 12, may suggest that there is reason to understand the story as divided into two parts rather than three. I will provide further discussion of this question later (in chapter 9); for now I wish only to draw attention to it as a question that needs reflection.

CHAPTER 7

Chapter 7 begins by confirming the suggestion made at the end of chapter 6: Ivan Ilich's death is a fact, acknowledged by all—friends, family, doctors, servants—including Ivan Ilich himself. The text suggests that Ivan Ilich's death is no longer a question, that "the whole interest he had for other people was whether he would soon vacate his place, and at last release the living from the discomfort caused by his presence, and be released himself from his sufferings" (151 [26:95]). As readers, we wonder what we ought to pay attention to now that Ivan Ilich's death has become a foregone conclusion.

The wretched quality of Ivan Ilich's life is emphasized in the description of the depressing effects of the drugs prescribed to deaden his pain, the tastelessness of the special foods prepared for him, and the shame he feels at being too weak to attend to the performance of his bodily functions without help. It is at this point that Tolstoy injects the first note of comfort into the steadily worsening condition of Ivan Ilich. He takes pleasure in the company of a servant named Gerasim who has been assigned the duty of assisting Ivan Ilich in using the commode. This is the same Gerasim who held Peter Ivanovich's coat for him at the end of chapter 1. He had reminded the unreceptive Peter Ivanovich that "all of us" would some day be in the same condition as the recently deceased Ivan Ilich.

Gerasim is young, strong, graceful, kindly, and radiant with life and health. He is full of sympathy for his dying master and not in the least offended or troubled by the nature of his task. On one occasion, after Gerasim has lifted Ivan Ilich's feet to place them on the seat of a chair, it seemed to Ivan Ilich that he felt a diminishment of pain. When Gerasim raises Ivan Ilich's feet still higher, it seems to Ivan Ilich that he feels no pain at all. Soon Gerasim begins to sit regularly with Ivan Ilich, supporting the sick man's feet on his shoulders. It is interesting to note that the last several references to this practice no longer mention the notion of the elevation of Ivan Ilich's legs as the source of comfort; attention is focused instead on the fact that Gerasim is supporting them. The suggestion is that Ivan Ilich, having been completely cut off from those close to him—family, friends, colleagues—by their indifference to and discomfort with his plight, here renews contact with a fellow human being. Since the isolation Ivan Ilich has experienced in his illness is shown to be only the last stage of a process that had been steadily developing throughout his life, his contact with Gerasim is doubly important. It signifies not only comfort for the terminally ill patient in his final weeks; it suggests also that a process that has characterized Ivan Ilich's behavior throughout his life may have begun to be reversed. Let us make use once again of the method of reading the apparently straightforward narrative metaphorically. Ivan Ilich's steady movement away from people, and theirs away from him, is here countered by the movement of Ivan Ilich and Gerasim toward one another and by their touching one another, by Gerasim's genuine sympathy for Ivan Ilich and by Ivan Ilich's acknowledging his need for this sympathy. This touch, this offer and acceptance of pity, may signify Ivan Ilich's first step away from the sense of total isolation and annihilation he experienced at the end of chapter 6. Tolstoy makes it clear that Gerasim also represents truthfulness by contrasting his willingness to admit and accept the fact that Ivan Ilich is dying with the insistence—by this time entirely hypocritical—of his family and friends that he is merely "sick." It is this "lying" that is most painful to Ivan Ilich, especially the presumption of his family and friends that he, too, should participate in the lie.

CHAPTER 8

Chapter 7 presents the one bright dimension of the life of the dying Ivan Ilich; chapter 8 is devoted to a description of the other dimensions, all of them uniformly dark and dismal. This description takes the form of an account of a day in the life of the dying protagonist. It begins with the note that Ivan Ilich knows the day has begun only because Gerasim, who is by now in the habit of passing the entire night with his master, has left. During the hours in which Gerasim is not present, Ivan Ilich's life is an undifferentiated round of suffering: "Whether it was morning or evening, Friday or Sunday made no difference, it was all just the same: the gnawing, unmitigated, agonizing pain, never ceasing for an instant, the consciousness of life inexorably waning, but not yet extinguished, the approach of that ever dreaded and hateful Death which was the only reality" (155 [26:99]).

Even though Ivan Ilich understands his situation, he sees that those around him expect him still to play the normal role for one of his position. He orders the servant to leave, but then, not wanting to be left alone, he recalls him on the pretext of needing help to take his medicine. As he takes the medicine he thinks again: Perhaps it will help? Having swallowed it, however, he knows that it will not. Finally, he orders tea to be brought, even though he doesn't want it, because he understands that the servant expects that in an orderly household "the masters would want their tea" (155 [26:98]). Ivan Ilich, left alone, groans "not so much with pain, terrible though that was, as from mental anguish" (154 [26:100]); he thinks, if only death would come more quickly—but then thinks again, anything is better than death (154 [26:100]).

The look of despair that Ivan Ilich directs at the servant causes the latter to start with perturbation. Seeing the servant's difficulty, Ivan Ilich proceeds through his entire routine: washes his face and hands, changes his shirt, brushes his teeth, combs his hair. He even feels better, until he actually tastes the tea that has been brought; thereupon the pain, the strange taste in his mouth, and the awareness of his impending death return once more. Tolstoy creates a portrait of one who is without hope, but who hopes, as it were, that he might hope.

Thus, he receives the doctor, and even listens to what the doctor has to say, just as he used "to submit to the speeches of the lawyers, though he knew very well that they were all lying, and knew why they were lying" (157 [26:101]). Ivan Ilich's pretense at falling in with the expectations of the situation is matched by that of his wife, who has decided that her proper role in the situation is to manifest the opinion that "he was not doing something that he ought to do and was himself to blame," while she "reproached him lovingly for this" (157 [26:102]). And so the day proceeds through an entire series of such encounters: the visit of still another specialist, his comfortless nap, his dinner, and a visit from his daughter and her fiancé. The situation is very well summed up by Ivan Ilich's reflections on his wife's behavior toward him: "He felt that he was surrounded and involved in such a mesh of falsity that it was hard to unravel anything. Everything she [Praskovya Fyodorovna] did for him was entirely for her own sake; she told him she was doing for herself what she actually was doing for herself, as if that was so incredible that he must understand the opposite" (157 [26:102]). His entire waking life—his daytime life—consists only of such incredibly intricate posturings and crazily complex deceits. The reader experiences a stark contrast between the "day" of chapter 8 and the "night" of the preceding chapter. Night, with the honest and kind Gerasim and the awareness that death is the issue, seems a much more genuine, brighter time than the day, with its indifferent, even inimical, visitors and the pretense that Ivan Ilich is merely sick.

It thus appears that "night," time of fear and dismay, is actually much superior to the apparent clarity and cheerfulness of "day." This may, in turn, lead to the notion that everything about Ivan Ilich's life needs to be understood as Praskovya Fyodorovna wanted her words to be understood—in reverse. If one begins to reason in this way, it is not far to the conclusion—already consciously reached by Ivan Ilich—that the apparent crisis in his life, the conflict between wellness and disease, should rather be understood as a crisis of life and death. Thus, during the night (chapter 7) Ivan Ilich is conscious that he faces a question of life and death, but during the following day (chapter 8) he is surrounded by the pretense that the question is one merely of health and sickness. It is this pretense that is, in fact, most painful to him. Reasoning still further, the "day," because it is so full of lying, posturing, pretense, and pain, is a far more painful time than the "night," which contains the comfort offered by the presence of Gerasim and the realization of the true nature of the question at issue. In this way it is suggested that the usual metaphorical values of "day" (bright, positive, optimistic, vital) should be understood as their opposites. Thus, the "normal" life of Ivan Ilich, as represented in the description given in chapter 8, is seen really to be tantamount to his death, and, by extension, the "normal" conceptions of life and death are portrayed as the reverse of the true conceptions. The "life" that Ivan Ilich has led (and continues to lead, as best he can, in chapter 8) is really his "death"; like Praskovya Fyodorovna's teasing banter, that ordinary life involves an incredibly complicated deception—to be understood aright, it must be understood in reverse. At this point we do well to recall the opening lines of chapter 2, the beginning of the story of the "life" of Ivan Ilich: "The past history of the life of Ivan Ilich was most simple and most ordinary, and most terrible" (129 [26:68]). Seen in the light cast by chapter 8, his life is, and has been, terrible indeed.

Chapter 8 ends with the description of the visit paid to Ivan Ilich by his wife, his daughter, and her suitor before they leave for the theater. It is clear, however, that the theatricals are already in progress while they are yet at home. All of them are unrelenting in their insistence that Ivan Ilich is merely indisposed. Conversation centers on everyday, mundane topics. The observant reader notices that the portion of the conversation in which the merits of the actress Sarah Bernhardt are discussed is more significant than it may appear to be, since the question at issue is the "realism of her acting" (159 [26:104]). At the very end, the little drama is interrupted by Ivan Ilich, who falls immovably silent and refuses to participate further. After an uncomfortably long silence, his visitors take their leave, going, as it were, from one performance to another.

Left alone, Ivan Ilich calls for Gerasim. Thus, the cycle of night and day, described in chapters 7 and 8, is now completed. The description shows Ivan Ilich still caught between two competing conceptions of his situation, conceptions that are "as different as night and day." With the end of chapter 8 we reach the end of the second portion of the novel, as suggested by our earlier consideration of chapter lengths. These four chapters have presented the illness of Ivan Ilich and its results. The next four (9 through 12) will center on his dying and death. As we embark on those final chapters, we should remember that some change has overtaken Ivan Ilich as his illness has grown worse over the course of the middle chapters of the novel. His daytime, ordinary life has grown increasingly hateful to him, and his appreciation of its nighttime complement has increased in proportion. We leave him at the end of chapter 8 on the threshold of the return of Gerasim, night, comfort, honesty, and truth. We would expect that in the next set of chapters an attempt will be made to show that truth.

8

Death

We come now to the consideration of the final four chapters of *The Death of Ivan Ilich*. Before we start, however, it will be well to summarize the material we have already covered. In the first four chapters of the novel Tolstoy presents the life of the protagonist from his childhood until the onset of his illness, a period of about 40 years. Chapters 5 through 8 present the development of the illness and its disastrous effects on the life Ivan Ilich has built for himself. We have noted that at the end of chapter 6 the protagonist is "as good as dead already"; indeed, one of the main functions of these central chapters is to create an awareness, both in Ivan Ilich and in the reader, of the important distinction between regarding the protagonist's situation as exemplary of the opposition "life versus death" or "health versus sickness." The conception "health versus sickness" is associated with the "ordinary," daytime life of Ivan Ilich, while "life versus death" is characteristic of his "new" life, occasioned by the suffering and debilitation of his illness and expressed most clearly during the hours of night and in the company of the servant Gerasim. Chapters 7 and 8 present a juxtaposed account of these two "lives" of Ivan Ilich: the nighttime life (with Gerasim) in chapter 7 and the daytime life (with family, doctors, visitors) in chapter 8. At the end of chapter 8, night has begun once again, and Ivan Ilich asks for Gerasim to be sent to him. This suggests that as we embark on the final chapters we may expect to find an emphasis on the new, nighttime life of Ivan Ilich and on the question of life and death associated with it.

CHAPTER 9

The opening paragraph of chapter 9 confirms the suggestion at the end of chapter 8: "His wife returned late at night. She came in on tiptoe, but he heard her, opened his eyes, and made haste to close them again. She wished to send Gerasim away and sit with him herself, but he opened his eyes and said: 'No. Go away' " (160 [26:105]). This little confrontation clearly illustrates the juxtaposition of opposites: daytime/nighttime; the ordinary ("old") life of Ivan Ilich/his life during his illness (his "new" life); his wife, Praskovya Fyodorovna/the servant, Gerasim; "health versus sickness"/"life versus death," and so on. This technique of the contrast of opposites is characteristic of Tolstoy's art at every stage of his career. One need only think of the title of his most famous novel, *War and Peace*, for an indication of this, and examples could be multiplied almost endlessly. Ivan Ilich's position at this stage of the novel is clearly one in which he must confront the various pairs of opposites that are before him and come to some resolution about them, to make his choice. As readers, we need to remember at this point that we, too, have been placed in this position. We have noted already that at the end of chapter 1 it is we, the readers, who are left with making the judgment that Peter Ivanovich decides is (metaphorically) "not within his jurisdiction."

Having symbolically decided (by sending his wife away) to devote himself to the "new life" side of the antinomies confronting him, Ivan Ilich has a dream that will prove to be quite significant for our understanding of the remainder of the text. Here is a literal translation of the Russian original: "It seemed to him that he was being painfully thrust into a narrow, deep black bag; he was being pushed in ever deeper, but he was unable to be pushed all the way in. And this action, which terrified him, was being accomplished with suffering. And he both feared and desired to fall into the bag all the way; he both struggled against this and tried to help it along. And then suddenly he broke through and fell, and he woke up. (26:105). The significance of this dream has been variously interpreted and will be discussed at some length in chapter 9 of this book.

Its immediate effect is to reduce Ivan Ilich to tears of self-pity and to an outcry against God's condemnation of him to a life of pain and suffering and His abandonment of him. He even sends Gerasim away. Once he is completely alone, however, something new happens to him. He falls silent, becomes closely attentive, and seems to sense a voice speaking to him not in words but from within himself, "the voice of his soul" (160 [26:106]). This voice asks Ivan Ilich what he wants, and Ivan answers, "To live and not to suffer. . . . to live as I used to, well and pleasantly" (161 [26:106]). When, however, Ivan Ilich calls the most pleasant moments of his life to mind, he finds them to have been not as pleasant as they had seemed. In fact, with the exception of some memories of childhood, he finds his past life to have been not really pleasant at all. The child he had been, however, is no more, and all that produced the person he now is seems trivial or even disgusting. He reviews, mentally, the entire course of his life and finds that "the further he departed from childhood and the nearer he came to the present the more worthless and doubtful were the joys" (161 [26:106]). His official duties he now thinks of as "dead work" (*mertvaia sluzhba*); he concludes that "the longer it lasted the more deadly it became" (161 [26:107]). His reflections suggest to him that the higher he rose in the opinion of those around him, the more he succeeded in his work, the more "life was ebbing away from [him]" (161 [26:107]).

It finally occurs to Ivan Ilich to think that perhaps he has not lived his life as he should, but this seems inconceivable to him: " 'But how could that be, when I did everything properly?' he replied, and immediately dismissed from his mind this, the sole solution of all the riddles of life and death, as something quite impossible" (161 [26:107]).

In this chapter Ivan Ilich finally becomes completely alone. He sends both his wife and Gerasim away, and he realizes consciously the loneliness of his position. In this state he begins to be aware of a voice speaking to him from within himself, and this voice encourages him to review his past and to judge whether or not he has lived rightly. This process of review and judgment will be continued in each of the succeeding chapters; Ivan Ilich will not, however, be able to appreciate the fact that he has lived wrongly until the final chapter of the novel. He will continue to resist this judgment on his past life, this "strange idea" as he calls it (162 [26:107]) until the very end.

CHAPTER 10

Tolstoy uses the beginning of this chapter to remind us that the time frame of the story and the parameters of its space are shrinking rapidly. "Two weeks" go by, and "Ivan Ilich now no longer left his sofa . . . facing the wall nearly all the time" (162 [26:107]). He reflects constantly on the "irresolvable" question before him ("Why this agony?"), irresolvable because the only possible resolution involves the conception that he has not lived rightly.

The notion, developed already in chapter 9, that Ivan Ilich is caught between two contrasting interpretations of his situation is confirmed in this chapter and stated directly: "His life had been divided between two contrary and alternating moods: either despair and the expectation of this uncomprehended and terrible death, or hope and an intently interested observation of the functioning of his organs" (162 [26:107–08]). Is it a question of life and death, or of health and sickness? The farther the illness progresses, however, the more "fantastic" and "unreal" the mood of hope seems to be, and the more insistent the mood of terror before death.

Ivan Ilich has in these two weeks come to exist almost exclusively within himself, in his memories of the past. As he lies with his face turned to the back of the sofa, he reviews his past life again and again. This process, which had begun in chapter 9, has now taken on a consistent and, as we shall see later, significant form. It always begins with the present and works backwards through time toward his childhood, the only point of light in the whole dismal story, and there it stops, because those memories, while pleasant, are also painful because the person he was then seems unrecoverable.

His reviewing of the past suggests to him not only that the closer he comes to childhood, the happier he was, but also that the farther back he goes into his memory, the more there was of life. Thus, it seems to him that the older he became, the more confirmed in the habits of his "ordinary" life, the less life there was and the more suffering. The immediate occasion of these thoughts is, of course, the illness from which he is suffering; however, in his reflections the change from life to death becomes generalized against the entire history of his life, not just against the history of his illness. This suggests that his "illness" has pervaded his entire life, from childhood on, and that the disease from which he currently suffers is a figurative expression of his general "illness" that has gotten steadily worse from the time he began ceasing to be the person he had been as a child. In the end, his reflections lead him to a general conclusion, couched not in terms of the history of his disease, but of the history of his life: "Life, a series of increasing sufferings, flies further and further towards its end—the most terrible suffering of all" (163 [26:109]).

Reflecting thus, it occurs to Ivan Ilich that, if there is no hope that life can be other than this entirely dismal process of graduated sufferings ending in dissolution, it would at least be some comfort to understand why this is so. But, as in chapter 9, Ivan Ilich is still unable to admit the thought that he has not lived right. On this occasion, however, the position is stated still more definitely: "An explanation would be possible if it could be said that I've not lived as I ought to. But it's impossible to say that" (163 [26:109]).

CHAPTER 11

Two weeks more elapse, during which the physiological condition of Ivan Ilich deteriorates still further. The chapter opens with Praskovya Fyodorovna's entrance into the study to inform Ivan Ilich that their daughter's suitor has made a formal proposal of marriage. Her announcement is never made, however, because she finds her husband in a sharply deteriorated condition and lying flat upon his back on the sofa, staring upward with fixed eyes and groaning in pain. Ivan Ilich directs a look of absolute hatred at his wife and tells her: "For Christ's sake, let me die in peace" (164 [26:109]). This is the first mention of the name of Christ in the text of the novel, and it appears as part of a cliché expression, which, however, in Russian is more of a plea than an imprecation. In accord with the strategy that has been adopted in reading the novel, we would expect the apparently innocent and natural invocation of Christ's name as part of a figure of speech to be masking a direct and literal reference. In thinking back over the preceding chapters we may well remember Ivan Ilich's outcry in chapter 9 about his aloneness and sense of abandonment, and about the apparent cruelty of God in allowing him to suffer so, about God's absence (160 [26:105–6]). Considering this passage in the light of the present mention of the name of Christ we cannot but note the similarity in substance between the thoughts of Ivan Ilich in chapter 9 and Christ's words delivered from the agony of the cross: "My God, my God, why hast Thou forsaken me?" Going back a little further, to the beginning of chapter 8, we may recall the passage "Morning or evening, *Friday or Sunday*, made no difference, it was all just the same." (155 [26:99]), italics mine) and note that Friday and Sunday were the two crucial days (Good Friday and Easter Sunday) in the biblical account of Christ's passion. These hints should serve to alert the reader to the possible presence of a biblical subtext in the novel; such a suspicion should come as no surprise, given Tolstoy's intense interest in the teaching of Christ at the time *The Death of Ivan Ilich* was written. There will be further discussion of this point in the section on chapter 12 of the novel.

Ivan Ilich greets the doctor with the same look of hatred he has directed against his wife and daughter. He commands the doctor, too, to leave him in peace and declares that the doctor can do nothing for him. Indeed, the doctor admits to Praskovya Fyodorovna that there is in fact no hope of recovery and that the final agony of the patient will be particularly terrible. The narrator, however, informs us that awful as the physical suffering has been and is, "worse than the physical sufferings were his mental sufferings which were his chief torture"

(164 [26:110]). This contrast of the physical (or physiological) with the moral (in the sense of "spiritual" rather than "ethical") comes as no surprise, either as an artistic device (we have noted earlier many examples of contrast in the text) or in the substance of the comparison. The contrast between the suffering occasioned by Ivan's physical illness and that brought on by the lying and hypocrisy required to maintain the fiction that he is merely sick when he is, in fact, dying has been repeatedly mentioned in the text. The present passage, however, is different in that it assigns definite categories to what were earlier called "the two moods" of Ivan Ilich. These categories, which I will refer to from here on as the "physiological" and the "spiritual," will become increasingly significant as the novel reaches its climax in chapter 12. I will discuss this point further in the last chapter of this book.

Ivan Ilich's spiritual suffering has, in addition, reached a new peak of intensity and a new center of focus. Formerly, this portion of his pain had been the result of the necessity he had felt to "keep up appearances" by cooperating in the general pretense that he was merely ill and, by following doctor's orders, would recover. Now we learn that his spiritual suffering has been occasioned by the thought, which occurred to him during the night before the morning described in chapter 11, "what if my whole life, my conscious life, has been 'wrong'?" (164 [26:110]). This is, of course, a very important admission on the part of Ivan Ilich, especially given his stout resistance to it as described in the preceding two chapters. The following passage contains another interesting suggestion: "It occurred to him that his scarcely perceptible attempts to struggle against what was considered good by the most highly placed people, those scarcely noticeable impulses which he had immediately suppressed, might have been the real thing, and all the rest false" (164 [26:110]). This passage suggests that we recall those instances in Ivan Ilich's life when he did what was "done" at the expense of what his sincere inclination dictated. The most notable of these instances is the discomfort he felt in participating in the youthful (presumably sexual) escapades of his fellow students; we remember that he ignored this feeling because he knew that "such actions were done by people of good position and that they did not regard them as wrong" (130 [26:70]). The effect of this passage is to confirm a suggestion we considered earlier: that the proper strategy to be followed in coming to an understanding of Ivan Ilich's life and death involves a preparedness to understand what we learn as its opposite or reverse. The main or generalized conclusion that this principle would suggest is that when we seem to be finding out about the "life" of Ivan Ilich we are actually finding out about his "death." And, conversely, that when his "death" (or his awareness, for example, that he is actually dying rather than simply ill) is at issue, he is in fact coming closer to "life." This thought is confirmed directly in the following passage: "In the morning, when he first saw his footman, then his wife, then his daughter, and then the doctor, their every word and movement confirmed the awful truth that had been revealed to him during the night. In them he saw himself—all that for which he had lived—and saw clearly that it was not real at all, but a terrible and huge deception *which had hidden both life and death [from him]*" (164 [26:110], italics mine).

Chapter 11 concludes with a momentary relapse by Ivan Ilich into the "other" mood, that "daytime" conception of hope for recovery and the conviction that his situation involves the question of health and sickness rather than life and death. This is brought about by his agreeing, at his wife's suggestion, to take communion. Confession and communion do indeed produce a momentarily beneficial effect. "He seemed to feel some relief from his doubts and, consequently, from his sufferings" (165 [26:111]). This relief proves to be short-lived, however; the comforting words spoken by his wife serve only to reinflame the hatred he had felt earlier in the day, and the chapter ends with his pain reaching a new and higher threshold. Ivan Ilich commands them all to "Get out!"

Chapter 11 has introduced no new dimension into our understanding of the novel, but it has sharpened and focused (sometimes, refocused) our grasp of the substance and technique of the story to this point. It seems to fulfill the function of preparing us as readers to deal with the complexities of the final, climactic chapter and its resolution of the enigma of the life and death of Ivan Ilich.

Chapter 12

The Death of Ivan Ilich has, in its first 11 chapters, brought its hero and its readers to the point of directly confronting death and of attempting to understand the significance of the hero's life and death. Chapter 12 begins with the problem of that significance having been clearly delineated, but with its solution still in doubt. The problem is this: has Ivan Ilich lived rightly or wrongly? Its delineation has advanced to the point that it seems clear to Ivan Ilich that if he *has* lived wrongly, his illness, his suffering, and his impending death can all be seen to make a sort of sense; if, however, he *has not* lived wrongly, then his life, suffering, and death make no sense at all. The uncertainty and doubt remain, however: "At the moment he answered his wife he realized that he was lost, that there was no return, that the end had come, the very end, and his doubts were still unsolved and remained doubts" (165–66 [26:112]).

It is the function of chapter 12 to resolve these doubts, and it is just this chapter that has seemed most problematical to readers of the novel. Often the resolution offered by Tolstoy strikes readers as simplistic or naive in the apparent (and too quick) triumph of Ivan Ilich over death. Since chapter 12 is so central to any general reading of the novel I am going to discuss it in the context of my concluding remarks, which are offered in the next chapter of this book. At this point I will discuss just one aspect of the final chapter, the manner in which it continues and completes the earlier suggestions of a connection between the death of Ivan Ilich and the passion of Christ.

As we have seen, *The Death of Ivan Ilich* is remarkable for the fact that what appears on its surface is often suggestive of complementary or contrastive connotations lying beneath that surface. We have examined the symbolism associated with such objects as furniture or card games. We have noted that very often it seems most appropriate to read what are evidently figures of speech as though they had a direct, literal significance and, conversely, to read what is apparently simple and direct as a metaphor. Occasionally, it has even seemed appropriate to see in words, phrases, or situations their exact opposites. What all of this suggests is that the text of the novel contains within it a number of subtexts, which both complement and compete with what is reported on the surface level.

One such suggestive pattern is the subtextual cluster of allusions to the motif of resurrection and to the Passion narrative that the story, especially its final chapter, contains. Ivan Ilich is, for example, described at one point as the *"phenix de la famille."* This metaphor is a mere cliché as it is used in chapter 2, and it seems to refer to nothing more than Ivan's superiority over his two brothers in intelligence, accomplishments, and what would be called today "career prospects." In chapter 12, however, this epithet, if the reader recalls it, is likely to seem exactly apt as Ivan's spirit, phoenix-like, escapes the pain and ruin of his dying body.

The story also contains a number of details that seem unremarkable when considered only in the context of the surface text. If, however, they are taken together, they comprise a cluster of allusions to the crucifixion of Jesus. For example: Ivan's final agony lasts three days (chapter 12); in chapter 9 he calls out to God, "Why do you torment me?" and weeps at "His cruelty and His absence," an echo of Christ's "My God, My God! Why hast Thou forsaken me?"; Ivan's dying commitment of his son to the care of Praskovya Fyodorovna (chapter 12) recalls another of Christ's last words, "Woman, behold thy son." The emphatic magnitude of Ivan's physical pain is hardly excessive[1] in the context of an implied comparison to the sufferings of death by crucifixion; both Jesus and Ivan are wounded in the side (Ivan's illness originates from a blow in the side suffered in a fall from a ladder [chapter 3]). At the end Ivan is sorry for those whom he had, with some reason, grown to hate. He has become aware that they are ignorant of the hypocrisy of their lives as he had been. His attempt to say "forgive" (chapter 12) can be read as a plea in their behalf as well as his own, suggesting a comparison with Christ's "Father, forgive them for they know not what they do." The family's ill-concealed complaints against the inconvenience represented by Ivan's condition are matched in the Passion account by the taunts directed at Jesus by the crowd. One of these is that Jesus saved others but was unable to save himself (Mk 15:31). Of Ivan, too, it is said that he is unable to save himself (chapter 12; 166 [26:112]). It should also be noted that this is said of Ivan Ilich in the context of a comparison between his position and that of someone "in the hands of the executioner," as was Christ (166 [26:112]).

Finally just before his death Ivan hears "someone above him" say "It is finished" (chapter 12; 167 [26:113]). The echo of the Passion narrative is obvious to the modern reader but was more obscure when the Russian original first appeared because the Gospel text (in the received Russian version of Tolstoy's time) employed the phrase "it is accomplished," instead. In his *A Harmonization and Translation of the Four Gospels*, however, Tolstoy emended the standard translation by replacing "it is accomplished" with "it is finished." The story's final chapter clearly suggests a connection between Ivan's demise and Christ's passion. Since Ivan escapes from the power of death at the end of the narrative, it seems appropriate to extend the comparison beyond the passion to the resurrection, especially as this is also suggested by the earlier comparison of Ivan to the mythological phoenix.

Thus, the mystery of the resurrection, which, like all the New Testament miracles, had no theological significance for Tolstoy and which he specifically excluded from his version of the Gospels, seems at the same time to have had a certain amount of importance for him as a motif suitable for artistic exploitation. It was used to good effect in contributing to the reader's appreciation of Ivan Ilich's new life in the spirit as artistically justified and aesthetically satisfying.

Chapter 12 of the novel appears to resolve the conflict in Ivan Ilich between the physiological and spiritual conceptions of life and death in favor of the latter. It seems to me, however, that this matter is not nearly as simple as the surface text may make it appear. The events of the last chapter, one of which is Ivan's dying claim that "death is finished" (167 [26:113]), need to be understood in the context of the novel as a whole and using the same strategies of interpretation as we have applied to the foregoing chapters. Such is the purpose of the next chapter of this study, wherein I will discuss the patterns and structures employed by Tolstoy in the organization of his text.

9

Pattern and Structure

Most readers of *The Death of Ivan Ilich* would probably agree with the view expressed by William Edgerton: "As we finish the story, we suddenly realize that its ending illuminates its title: the meaningless physical life of Ivan Ilich was really his death, and his physical death marked the beginning of his spiritual life beyond time and space" (Edgerton, 300).

Many students of the story, however, have been uncomfortable with this conclusion. They can accept that Tolstoy wanted his readers to understand that Ivan Ilich had lived wrongly, but they question his success in portraying the protagonist's last-minute "conversion" and regard it as inconsistent with the other elements of the story. There is an apparent lack of harmony between the pain and anxiety of Ivan's approach to death throughout the first 11½ chapters and their sudden disappearance at the end of the twelfth when he dies. A narrative that consistently bears Ivan toward death ends by delivering him into new life. Even such an ardent admirer as Mark Aldanov wonders whether Tolstoy has "really succeeded in bridging the chasm of death." According to Aldanov, Tolstoy's twofold purpose is "first to frighten the reader with death and then to reconcile him to it." He succeeds so well with the first that he proves unable to realize the second.[1]

Critics seem to have assumed that Tolstoy published the story in the pious hope that it would have a beneficial effect despite this flaw. It is possible, however, that Tolstoy had taken care to deal with the problem. In this chapter we will discuss the extent to which the discontinuity, apparent on the story's surface (hereafter, the *text*), between the main body of the narrative and its conclusion is resolved at deeper levels of its structure (the *subtexts*). These latter include a network of examples of *reversal*, a subtextual pattern of organization that contrasts with that of the text, and a subtle, sometimes ambiguous, use of symbolism. The various subtexts interact with the text to realize, if not intellectually, at least artistically, the transformation of death into life for which the novel is remarkable.

We have already discussed (in chapter 4) the apparent linearity of the surface structure of the novel. The decreasing lengths of the chapters, the way that they represent the steadily narrowing parameters of time and space, and the manner in which the story's content seems so neatly to divide itself into the three distinct phases of health, sickness, and death, all of these combine to produce the impression of a steadily progressing, ever narrowing fictional world in which the hero might well feel that he is like a "stone falling downwards with increasing velocity" (163 [26:109]) toward an inevitable collision with the ground. The apparently ineluctable linearity of the novel's surface, however, is counterbalanced by a variety of competing patterns lying beneath it.

The most obvious of these subtexts may be described as a network of reversals. The transference of events following the death of Ivan Ilich from their chronological position at the end of the story to the beginning of chapter 1 is the first reversal of which the reader becomes aware. This is soon followed by the discovery that the story is mainly devoted, not to Ivan Ilich's death (as suggested by the title), but to his life. This leads in turn to the realization that the very concepts of life and death have been reversed. The story contains other sudden reversals: the rapid change from success to failure to success in Ivan's career (chapter 3) and from health to disease (chapter 4). The interplay between Gerasim and Praskovya Fyodorovna (chapters 7 and 8) and Ivan's oscillations between hope and despair (especially chapter 10) may also be mentioned as examples of polarity and reversal rather than linearity and progression.

The motif of reversal is further developed by the recurrence of certain verbal formulations. In chapter 9, for instance, the thought occurs to Ivan that "it is as if I had been going downhill while I imagined I was going up" (161[26:107]), that is, that his true direction was the reverse of his apparent direction and, by extension, perhaps, that there is a subtextual direction in the story that is contrary to that of its surface text. The significance of this motif is confirmed by its reiteration in chapter 12: "What had happened to [Ivan] was like the sensation one sometimes experiences in a railway carriage when one thinks one is going backwards while one is really going forwards and suddenly becomes aware of the real direction" (166 [26:112]).[2]

A third aspect of the subtext of reversal concerns the valuation put on Ivan Ilich's changing moods. Sometimes he is full of the hope that he is merely ill and that he can, by carefully following a prescribed regimen, recover. At other times he experiences despair in the realization that he is dying. The reader naturally expects Ivan's spirits to rise when hope is in the ascendant and to decline when he is possessed by despair. Just so his spirits are relatively high in chapter 4 as he takes the approved steps to fight his disease, and just so they decline in chapters 5 and 6 as he begins to recognize that his illness is a mask for death. Throughout the first six chapters of the novel hope is fairly consistently associated with the hours of daylight, despair with darkness. (Note Ivan Ilich's frantic attempt to light a candle when he awakens in the dark in chapter 5.)

In chapter 7, however, Ivan's spirits rise (or is it that his spirit rises?) even though the scene takes place at night and he is in the company of the candid Gerasim who, unlike Ivan's relatives, makes no attempt to conceal the fact that he is very seriously ill and is, in fact, dying. This reversal continues in chapter 8, the action of which occurs during the hours of daylight. Ivan is surrounded throughout by the representatives of "hope"—his wife, family, doctors—but his spirits decline radically nonetheless. The relative comfort of the night described in chapter 7 is replaced by intense physical and emotional suffering.

These reversals in the expected emotional state of the hero suggest that there is a line of demarcation between chapters 6 and 7. In chapter 6 and before, hope is positive and despair negative. In chapter 7 and 8 these values are reversed, suggesting that Ivan's hope has been false and his despair misdirected. The pattern of reversal reappears in chapters 11 and 12. Chapter 11 presents a recurrence of the hopeful mood (Ivan's last communion), which culminates in a plunging of his spirits, while chapter 12 commences with an agonized despair that is ultimately converted into a euphoric and luminous epiphany.

The placement of this last aspect of reversal is particularly significant for the present analysis because it suggests a division of the story into two parts, separating the first six chapters from the last six. This halving of the story in turn suggests the existence of a subtextual principle of organization, which appears to be operating in competition with the surface organization. In contrast with the linear presentation of Ivan's illness, which divides the text into thirds, the embedded pattern, which may be styled "two-directional" or "reversing," provides the structural basis for the presentation of the other factor that bids for Ivan's attention: the question of life and death.

Seen in this perspective, the contents of the chapters appear in a different light. Chapters 2 through 6 now seem to represent an account of Ivan's gradual reduction from freedom to bondage, strength to weakness, community to isolation, and, indeed, from life to death, since in chapter 6 Ivan sees death "looking at him from behind the flowers" in the parlor (151[26:95]). At the end of chapter 6 there is nothing left for Ivan to do but "to look at [death] and grow cold" (151[26:95]; the Maude translation has "shudder" instead of "grow cold"). In terms of the story's linear surface, of course, these processes of reduction continue to intensify until the end of the work, but it is important to note that they are all virtually complete by the end of chapter 6. In the first half of that chapter Ivan still enjoys the freedom of his home and even returns periodically to work; from chapter 7 on, however, he is confined to his study. The strength implied by his freedom of movement in chapter 6 is replaced by weakness so extreme in chapter 7 that he requires assistance even to use the commode. In chapter 6 Ivan still participated in the life of his office and of his family, but in chapter 7 he is cut off from them completely by their conviction that he is, for practical purposes, already dead and that his continued existence is merely a troublesome inconvenience. His isolation is complete in all but the most superficial sense, and the passage in chapter 10 that describes him as being more alone than if he were "at the bottom of the sea or in the earth" hints at his death and burial and so continues the motif of the cooling corpse evoked in the last line of chapter 6.

Thus, the isolation, alienation, and even the "death" of the protagonist are already accomplished by the beginning of chapter 7. What, then, is the role of the last six chapters? I suggest that their primary artistic significance lies in the preparation they provide for the apparently miraculous reversal with which the story ends. If chapters 1 through 6 present an account of Ivan's "death," then chapters 7 through 12 depict his rebirth into a new "life." His isolation and alienation come to an end; he is freed of his anxiety over the meaning of his physical sufferings; he escapes the constrictions of time, space, and his own self-imposed limits; finally, he evades the power of death. Each of these factors is anticipated in the course of the last six chapters.

Chapter 7 brings the first hint of the possibility of Ivan's escaping from the isolation that he has himself established and that has been confirmed by the callous indifference of his family and friends. In Gerasim he finds a sincere and truthful contact with the world around him. He is comforted by Gerasim's presence and finds relief in his touch: Gerasim supports Ivan's upraised legs on his shoulders and "Ivan Ilych thought that in that position he did not feel any pain at all" (153 [26:97]). The comfort of physical contact recurs at the moment of Ivan's conversion, which is simultaneous with his son's grasping of his upraised hand (166 [26:112]). Likewise, Ivan's escape from the power of death is anticipated in the dream of the black bag in chapter 9. One of the symbolic referents of this image is certainly death, and Ivan's attitude towards the black bag is ambivalent from the first. In his dream he is torn between a desire to resist the force that is thrusting him ever deeper into the darkness and a desire to "fall right in." When, in chapter 12, Ivan experiences the seemingly incompatible torments of being thrust into a "black hole" and of being unable to "clamber right into it," his ambivalence comes as no surprise; nor does his eventual breakthrough ("he fell through and saw light"), which is also anticipated in the dream.

Perhaps the most striking of the anticipations of the story's outcome are those that prepare the way for the idea of escape from the shrinkage of space and time and, by extension, from the consequences of the improper life that Ivan has led. In chapter 10 we learn that "lately . . . during that terrible loneliness Ivan Ilych had lived only in memories of the past" (162 [26:108]). His recourse to reminiscence is in harmony with his decision "to think everything through again" (chapter 5). There, and in chapter 6, where this "rethinking" is repeated, the course of thought is forward, from the beginning of Ivan's illness to his present condition. In each of the last four chapters this motif returns, but now he begins with the present and moves steadily backward (the reverse of the order of his earlier "rethinkings") until he reaches his childhood (he reviews his whole life, not just the period of his illness), which seems to him to be "the one bright spot" (163 [26:109]) in an existence that is otherwise "ever blacker and blacker." In returning to the past Ivan causes time to run backwards and so cancels the direction in which he has been going. The luminescence of his memory of childhood, which he is able to recover in imagination, anticipates the dimensionless region of light, which is the figurative expression of his ultimate recovery. If chapters 2 through 6 are an account of his temporal progress toward death, chapters 7 through 12 develop the motif of temporal regress through which he recaptures his spiritual life.[3] Thus, while the text is the vehicle of Ivan's temporal, spatial, and physiological movement from birth to death, its subtext is the vehicle of his spiritual, nonspatial, and atemporal progress from death to rebirth.

It is in chapter 12 that we find the coalescence of these two principles. Following his emergence into the light and the reestablishment of his connection with his family, Ivan tries to express his repentance by saying "forgive" (in Russian *prosti*) but produces instead the word "forego" (in the Maude translation; literally, "pass through," in

Russian *propusti*). The blending of these two words marks the unification of the two themes and the two principles of organization. The desire for forgiveness, with its implication that Ivan has reached a new understanding of life by accepting at last that his life has been "wrong," merges with his acceptance of physiological death, and the gap between his desire to say *prosti* and his actually saying *propusti* is resolved in the remark that "he [or "He"] who needs to understand, will" (167 [26:113]. The verbal sign of the new life (*prosti*) is embedded in the verbal sign of the acceptance of the end of the old life (*propusti*), just as the story's subtextual (two-directional) structure is cloaked by, yet breaks through, the linear organization that characterizes its surface text. It is as though Ivan cannot say other than *propusti* because speech is a physiological act. The spiritual *prosti*, however, emerges from it nonetheless, for those who need to be aware of it. This includes, of course, the readers of the novel, who have accepted the implicit obligation of coming to a right understanding of the significance of the life and death of the protagonist.

The two levels of the story and their ultimate unification are also suggested by the ambiguously symbolic use of the image of the black bag. This twice-mentioned (chapter 9 and chapter 12) motif has generally been understood as suggesting a "womb"; Ivan's pain and struggling within it and his ultimate emergence from it into the light have consequently been seen as the trauma of his birth into a new life. Boris Sorokin, however, has cogently argued that the black bag refers rather to the intestinal tract (specifically, the blind gut, which Ivan suspects as a cause of his illness). In the light of the present analysis it becomes plain that both the physiological (elimination) and the spiritual (rebirth) interpretations of the symbolism are appropriate.

This study of *The Death of Ivan Ilich* does not represent a radical reinterpretation of the story's meaning; there are, in fact, few stories whose intended meaning is so abundantly clear. The attempt has been, rather, to describe the extent to which and the manner in which this meaning is artistically realized in the work. The complexity of the novel's structure has been illustrated by demonstrating the presence within it of a number of subtexts (thematic, organizational, symbolic, allusive), which has led, I hope, to an appreciation of the artistic fitness of the conclusion. The apparently miraculous conversion of the dying Ivan and his discovery of a new understanding of life at the end of the story are adequately prepared for by and artistically consistent with the preceding text.

The discussion in this and the preceding chapters has been intended to provide a reading of *The Death of Ivan Ilich* that both does justice to the nuanced complexity of the text and yet honors Tolstoy's earnest commitment to the view of literary art as a means for bringing important truths to the attention of the reader. I have sought, in other words, to read the novel in a manner consistent with its author's known intentions. I have devoted the bulk of my reading to an examination of the structural and stylistic means Tolstoy used to achieve the effects he intended. I hope that in this chapter I have managed to show that the novel's devices are adequate to and commensurate with those intentions. But what of the specific conceptions that my analysis has suggested Tolstoy intended to convey to his readers? Can we as readers of the novel be assured that the understanding of the nature and meaning of life and death, of the physiological and the spiritual, of health and disease, of suffering, isolation, alienation, and communion is congruent with that espoused by Tolstoy in other writings of this period? In short, we must address the question of whether the themes that this reading of *The Death of Ivan Ilich* has established as central to the novel were in fact central to Tolstoy's system of beliefs. It is to this question that we turn in the final chapter of this book.

10

Themes and Confirmations

The preceding several chapters have gone at some length into the style, structure, imagery, and narrative strategy of Tolstoy's most-celebrated fictional treatment of the theme of death. In this chapter I want to explore this theme, and others related to it, in greater detail by examining the connections between *The Death of Ivan Ilich* and other works by Tolstoy, whether fictional or not, that also deal with the theme of death.

The theme of death is ubiquitous in Tolstoy's writings, and, given that Tolstoy regarded the function of art and the mission of the artist as communicative, it behooves the reader of *The Death of Ivan Ilich* to be aware of the author's other pronouncements on this theme. *The Death of Ivan Ilich* is but one of numerous texts by Tolstoy on the subject of death, and our approach to it as a specific text cannot but be enriched by an acquaintance with some of these other writings. Such an acquaintance will show whether the particular nuances of the treatment of the theme of death that have emerged from our earlier consideration of the style and structure of the novel are or are not congruent with Tolstoy's other discussions of this theme. At the same time, it may well prove possible to refer specific images, strategies, or structural features of the novel to the explanatory context of other writings and thereby improve our understanding of their significance in *The Death of Ivan Ilich*. This approach is in accord with an important current line in research into Tolstoy's works, best represented by Richard Gustafson's recent *Leo Tolstoy: Resident and Stranger*. Gustafson shows again and again the considerable extent to which Tolstoy's personal reflections on philosophy and religion and the substance of his nonfictional writings form the basis of later fictional elaborations of the same themes.

There are various connections between *The Death of Ivan Ilich* and Tolstoy's earlier works. These connections are primarily thematic, centering on Tolstoy's continuing concern with death. His vision of the power of death, in fact, predates even his absorption in this subject at the time of *A Confession*, discussed earlier. Scholars have long recognized that the theme of death and the search for a compromise with its nullifying power is characteristic of Tolstoy at every stage of his career.[1] *War and Peace*, written son.c 20 years before *The Death of Ivan Ilich*, exemplifies Tolstoy's confrontation with the theme of death in the period prior to his crisis of the mid-1870s. The shock and confusion produced by death is suggested by the frequent recurrence of the question "what for?" in that novel. The sheer terror of death is represented most clearly, perhaps, in the reaction of the cynical and tough-minded courtier Vasilii Kuragin to the death of an acquaintance: " 'Ah, my friend,' " said he . . . and there was in his voice a sincerity and weakness which Pierre had never observed in it before. 'How often we sin, how much we deceive, and all for what? I am near sixty, dear friend. . . . All will end in death, all! Death is awful! . . .' And he burst into tears" (9:104).[2] This is, in essence, the power of the vision of death for Tolstoy. It is not just that death exists, it is the thought, "I, too, will die."[3]

Those who suffer or observe death in Tolstoy's works experience a multiplicity of emotional responses, ranging from terror through indifference to relief or joy. These responses are accompanied by various attempts to mitigate the awfulness of death: replacement of the dying or dead with the newly born or the promise of birth (the death of Prince Andrey's wife, Liza, in *War and Peace*; the death of Levin's brother, Nikolai, in *Anna Karenina*); patient recognition of the inevitability of death (the character of Eroshka in *The Cossacks*; the character of "Uncle" in *War and Peace*); a welcoming of death as the end of the sad limitations of corporeal life (the deathbed musings of Prince Andrey in *War and Peace*); and the belief that death is an appearance only, and not a reality (the character of Platon Karataev in *War and Peace*).

We have noted earlier (in chapter 1) that the problem of death became especially troublesome for Tolstoy in the 1870s and that his elaboration of the message of Christianity was in great part an answer to the challenge of death. It is clear that we must read *The Death of Ivan Ilich* in the context of the history of, and as the sequel to, Tolstoy's preoccupation with death and his attempts to answer its challenge. It is less clear whether the novel is to be seen as an exemplification of Tolstoy's ultimate solution of the problem of death or as one of the anxiety-ridden stimuli that caused him to elaborate further upon that solution; that is, we face the question of whether the novel is an affirmation of the power of life over death or a cry of despair at the hopelessness of the human position. The account of existing scholarship on the work provided in chapter 3 of this book shows that the novel has been read in both of these ways.

The new view of life and death that emerged from Tolstoy's study of the Gospels is explained most completely in a series of treatises and tracts that he wrote between 1878 and 1882. I have discussed these briefly in an earlier chapter. Their function was to provide a more or less complete codification of the principles of Tolstoy's philosophy of life (or "religion," as he customarily referred to it) and a demonstration that these principles were all clearly derivable from the texts of the Gospels, when properly understood. In the decade following the completion of this series (*A Confession, A Critique of Dogmatic Theology, A Harmonization and Translation of the Four Gospels*, and *What I Believe*) Tolstoy wrote numerous other works (stories, plays, and short novels, as well as essays and tracts) in which various points of his doctrine were elaborated more fully. In the middle of this decade he wrote *The Death of Ivan Ilich*. We turn now to a consideration of two of these other works with a brief discussion of a third; we will attempt to discern the relationships among them and the connections they have with *The Death of Ivan Ilich*. These works are *The Gospel in Brief,*[4] with a brief excursus on the short novel *Master and Man,* and *On Life*. In considering the first we shall discover evidence of the general philosophical and religious views that preceded and seem to inform the writing of *The Death of Ivan Ilich*. In *On Life,* which followed the novel almost immediately, we shall find a large number of specific connections with *The Death of Ivan Ilich,* many with considerable value as glosses on the text of the novel. This will allow us to speak of a relationship between *The Death of Ivan Ilich* and *On Life* in which it seems that *On Life,* to some degree at least, offers a philosophical discussion of concepts that had been represented artistically in the novel first. Thus, there would appear to be a progression from general ideas expressed in an overtly religious context (*The Gospel in Brief*) to an artistically specific realization of these ideas (*The Death of Ivan Ilich*) to a more complete and philosophical rationalization, or even a codification, of these ideas in *On Life*.

The Gospel in Brief

The weightiest of the four volumes that Tolstoy wrote in explanation of his newfound religious beliefs between 1878 and 1882 was a ponderous work of biblical exegesis he called *A Harmonization and Translation of the Four Gospels*. A Gospel *harmony* attempts to conflate the reports of Christ's life on earth as recorded in the Gospels into a single narrative that draws upon the information presented in the Gospels as required by the biographical/chronological plan of the work being composed. Very often a Gospel harmony will make use of only the first three Gospels (Matthew, Mark, and Luke; the so-called synoptic Gospels) because these writings are evidently more biographical and less overtly theological in their intent than the fourth canonical gospel, the Gospel of John. Having chosen to use either three or all four Gospels, the harmonist compares them with one another and attempts to create as complete as possible a portrait of the actual chronological life of Jesus, including in their proper place all events imputed to that life whether a particular event is reported by only one or by more than one of the evangelists. Such conflations of the texts of the Gospels have been presented either as a single running account, which tends to blur the distinctions among the reports of the various evangelists, or in a format that attempts to preserve the distinctions among the subsidiary accounts, also known as a *parallel Gospel.*

Tolstoy's *A Harmonization and Translation of the Four Gospels* is a harmony of the first type; the texts of the four Gospels are combined into a single narrative. When more than one account of a particular event is available, Tolstoy either chooses one as the best or combines elements from one or more of the Gospel accounts to produce what he considers to be the best reading of the event. Tolstoy felt free to leave out certain parts of the Gospel accounts on the grounds of their irrelevance or unreliability. He wanted above all to produce an account of the *teaching* of Jesus that would be consistent within itself and also uniformly in accord with what Tolstoy believed to be the underlying precepts of Jesus' teaching.

A Harmonization and Translation of the Four Gospels, as its title suggests, offers not only an arrangement of the Gospel accounts of the life of Jesus (which were originally written and preserved in the so-called Koine Greek language) into a single narrative, but a translation of this arrangement from Greek into modern Russian as well. This translation, representing only a small percentage of the considerable bulk of *A Harmonization and Translation of the Four Gospels* as a whole, forms the substance of *The Gospel in Brief. The Gospel in Brief*, then, is an account of the life and teachings of Jesus, based upon the study, emendation, and conflation of the original Greek texts, freely edited by Tolstoy according to his own view and understanding of the Christian teaching and translated into modern Russian. The work purports to be not merely a harmony of the Gospels, but rather a single narrative account of the life and teaching of Jesus that approaches as closely as possible the original substance of that teaching (as Tolstoy understood it) and distances itself as far as possible from the errors about and misinterpretations (or "perversions" as Tolstoy preferred to call them) of that teaching that 1900 years of institutional church history had introduced into it.

Themes and Confirmations

A professional scholar of the Bible would be very unlikely to find Tolstoy's methods of harmonization appropriate, rigorous, justifiable, or capable of producing a creditable harmony. Tolstoy, however, was little troubled by the cavils of scholars. For our purposes, too, these are secondary considerations. What we need to know about *The Gospel in Brief* is what bearing its content and structure may have upon our reading of *The Death of Ivan Ilich*, which Tolstoy was to write some four years after he finished extracting *The Gospel in Brief* from the larger *A Harmonization and Translation of the Four Gospels.*

The central task of *The Gospel in Brief* would seem to have been to represent, as completely as possible within the confines of the preserved records of Jesus' life, the teaching of Christ as Tolstoy understood it. The work presents most of the basic conceptions about human life and the place of the human being within the universe that were to reappear later in the narrative and images of the novel. For example, the concept that human life involves a dual plane of existence emerges directly in *The Gospel in Brief*, where one of the chapters is titled "The Victory of the Spirit over the Flesh," but is only implied in *The Death of Ivan Ilich*. *The Gospel in Brief* refers directly to the divine and the human, the spirit and the flesh, the mind and the body; in the novel it is the implied task of Ivan Ilich to attempt to come to terms with these very dichotomies while dealing directly with the dichotomies of health/disease and life/death.

Jesus is represented as a human being who happened, for whatever reason, to be much more closely in touch with God's will for human life and behavior than the ordinary person. Thus, Jesus is, in Tolstoy's account of him, not a deity, but he is just as certainly not an ordinary person, either. In this, Tolstoy's Jesus is quite unlike Ivan Ilich, who is mainly remarkable for the fact that he is a completely ordinary person and his story a very common one.

Yet, the story of Jesus in *The Gospel in Brief* is a life story, the chronology of which is radically foreshortened in its early stages and maximally extended in its final phase. Exactly this can also be said, of course, of the story of Ivan Ilich. The courses of these two lives are quite different in most details, but they coincide in the agonized suffering that overcomes each of them at the end of his life. It may also be notable that both *The Death of Ivan Ilich* and *The Gospel in Brief* are divided into 12 chapters. The artfulness of the construction of the novel may not immediately be reflected in the naively straightforward narrative of *The Gospel in Brief*, but this impression can hardly be maintained once the reader has discovered that each of the 12 chapters of *The Gospel in Brief* turns out (much to his own surprise, ingenuously affirmed the author) to be neatly summarized by and subsumable under one of the 12 petitions of the Lord's Prayer in their proper order.

There is, then, a suggestion that the figure of Jesus in *The Gospel in Brief* is in some manner a counterpart to the figure of Ivan Ilich in the novel. I have discussed some of the more evident of the correspondences between the two in my reading of the novel's last chapter. The essence of the connection between Jesus and Ivan Ilich, however, seems to me to reside mainly in their mutual suffering and through that suffering their coming to understand more perfectly what it means to be a human being. Their mutual fate seems to suggest that the passage to full spiritual awareness cannot ever be traversed without suffering, whether the traveler is as remarkable as Jesus or as common as Ivan Ilich.

Is, then, the protagonist of *The Death of Ivan Ilich* to be regarded as a "Christ figure"? It would not be surprising to find that Tolstoy in this period of his life, centered as it was on the life and teaching of Jesus, looked to Christ as a model of human behavior; it *is* surprising, perhaps, to find indications that he associated so apparently pedestrian a character as Ivan Ilich with this model. And yet, Ivan Ilich is by no means the only character with whom Tolstoy seems to have dealt in this way; it may be useful to consider another of his later short novels, *Master and Man* (*Khoziain i rabotnik*, 1895) in this connection.

•   •   •

Master and Man is the story of a well-to-do, materialistic, and self-satisfied entrepreneur, Vasilii Andreevich, who sets off through a blizzard, accompanied by his hired workman, Nikita, in order to complete the final arrangements for a business deal. During the course of the terrible night that these two spend together in the open at the mercy of the storm, Vasilii Andreevich comes to see the error of his materialist and mercantile ways. He undergoes a conversion of sorts, and in the end he loses his own life while saving Nikita's. All of this, of course, sounds rather familiar to the reader of *The Death of Ivan Ilich*: the self-satisfied, materialistic protagonist; the poor but pious representative of the lower classes; the confrontation with the inevitable approach of death; and the last minute change of heart and renunciation of the former mode of life.

That Vasilii Andreevich, in effect, lays down his life for the sake of Nikita is only the most striking of the numerous parallels between his story in *Master and Man* and that of Jesus in the Passion narrative. We cannot fail to note, further, that it is the "master" who gives himself for the "man," and that Vasilii Andreevich lives in a village called "Kresty" (i.e., "The Crosses"). Numerous other details in the novel corroborate the suggestions implied by those just mentioned. Thus, while passing and repassing the entrance to a village, Vasilii Andreevich and Nikita notice that a shirt has been left hanging on a clothesline with its arms outstretched. As Vasilii Andreevich shivers through the night waiting for dawn and the end of the storm, he imagines, on three separate occasions, that he hears the crowing of a cock. As he rushes frantically about searching for the lost road, he encounters a hedgerow of wormwood. Finally, when the two travelers are discovered the following morning by a party of peasants, it turns out that the body of Vasilii Andreevich has frozen solid with its arms outstretched (much like the shirt on the clothesline) in a cruciform position. The parallel between Vasilii Andreevich and Christ can hardly be missed, and it is obviously the Christ of the Passion narrative that Tolstoy has in mind.

The extent of the allusions to the Passion story in *Master and Man* is even more striking if we compare the text of this work with that of its partial prototype, a story called "The Snowstorm" ("Metel' "), which Tolstoy wrote in 1856. "The Snowstorm" is based upon the same general situation as *Master and Man*—a dangerous journey undertaken at night through a blizzard. *Master and Man* even repeats many of the details contained in its predecessor: the description of the wind and the specification of its direction, the ability of the horses to find their own way home if not misdirected by their drivers, the advice (which goes unheeded) not to travel through the storm, the motif of the village as a refuge, and the repeated refusal of the protagonist to avail himself of that refuge. Yet it is clear that in *Master and Man* Tolstoy has invested this material with a completely different artistic force and suggestiveness. "The Snowstorm" uses the journey through the storm as a framework within which to examine the emotions (mainly fear) of the protagonist and to describe the curious operations of the mind with respect to the evocation of memories of the past through association with the experiences of the present. "The Snowstorm," in short, describes a real storm (Tolstoy himself had an experience of the kind reported in the story) and its potential effects on the psyche of an individual person.

Master and Man, on the other hand, uses this same material to epitomize man's life story as a whole, the tension between the spiritual and material ego within the individual, and man's ultimate spiritual resurrection "accompanied by the loss of his material being." "The Snowstorm" describes the journey of a particular young officer who is traveling home; *Master and Man* is rather the story of Man's journey to his spiritual home. The story ends with the death of Vasilii Andreevich, but this death is portrayed as a victory, as a resurrection or new birth of Vasilii Andreevich's almost extinct soul. Thus, the novel contains not only numerous allusions to Christ's passion, but, in suggesting (by the cruciform position of his arms and legs) that Vasilii Andreevich is a Christ figure, the novel draws upon the Christian reader's awareness of Christ's physical resurrection as a confirmation of Vasilii Andreevich's spiritual one. At the same time, of course, the comparison may suggest that the achievement of one's own spiritual resurrection is of greater moment than belief in Christ's physical resurrection, a point of Christian dogma that Tolstoy stoutly and consistently denied.

The figures of Vasilii Andreevich and Ivan Ilich have so much in common that if it can be shown with absolute clarity that Tolstoy intended Vasilii Andreevich as a Christ figure, then it is not particularly difficult to see Ivan Ilich in the same light, given the numerous (if more subtle) references to the story of Christ's passion in *The Death of Ivan Ilich*.

On Life

Tolstoy began to write the lengthy treatise *On life* (*O zhizni*, 1886–88) in the months immediately following the completion of *The Death of Ivan Ilich*. In light of the content of *The Death of Ivan Ilich*, the circumstances surrounding the composition of *On Life* seem particularly remarkable, and I will therefore report them briefly here.

Tolstoy made his last corrections to the text of the novel at the end of March 1886. In the summer of that same year (probably in early August) Tolstoy had an accident. While helping a peasant widow on his estate to cart hay, he hurt his leg by bumping it painfully against the wagon. In her *Memoirs* Tolstoy's wife, Sofia Andreevna, described this injury using the Russian word *ushib*, by a strange coincidence the same word Tolstoy used to describe the fall from the ladder and blow to the side that seemed to be the cause of Ivan Ilich's terminal illness.[5] As was the case with Ivan Ilich, from a seemingly insignificant beginning Tolstoy's condition gradually worsened. By the middle of August, as we learn from one of Mrs. Tolstoy's letters, he had been confined to bed for more than a week suffering from fever, nausea, and constant pain in his injured leg.[6] Whether or not connected with the apparent fact that his life seemed to be imitating his art with uncomfortable precision, Tolstoy's thoughts turned to gloomy reflections on his own mortality, and, again much in the manner of Ivan Ilich, he "thought the matter through from the beginning."

Not long thereafter he was visited by a certain Anna Diterikhs, a young woman who would later become the wife of Vladimir Chertkov, the most prominent of Tolstoy's disciples. She pressed him to formulate his ideas on the subject of life and death for her instruction. His promise to do so led him into a task that would occupy him off and on for nearly two years; *On Life* was finally published in the edition of Tolstoy's collected works that appeared in 1888.[7]

On Life is Tolstoy's most philosophical work in the sense that of all the major nonfiction writings of the last 30 years of his life it resorts least to the authority of Jesus and the Scriptures in advancing its arguments. Tolstoy offered it as a purely rational investigation of the nature of human life and of such familiar concerns of the human condition as the sources of contentment and happiness, questions of right conduct and behavior, and the existence of evil in the form of illness, suffering, and death.

Tolstoy's concept of life is decidedly dualistic.[8] He contends that there ought to be a distinction made between "human life" and the "animal life of man." The "mere existence" characteristic of the animal (physical) body is contrasted to the "true life" of the spirit. The body is considered transient and ultimately unimportant in comparison with the spirit. The spirit is incorporeal, impersonal, and unassailable by any external force. Within the logic of Tolstoy's reasoning even the death of the body is of no moment, since it affects only the ephemeral, animal existence and leaves untouched the true life of the spirit. He portrays happiness, contentment, right conduct, and imperishability as the essential characteristics of the person who understands and acts upon the primacy of this true, spiritual, human life; unhappiness, wrong conduct, suffering, and death, however, are the lot of the person who makes the mistake of treating the "animal life" as though it were of primary value.

The distinctions and conclusions offered by Tolstoy in *On Life*, not surprisingly, mesh very well with those we have noted in *The Gospel in Brief*, and, like so much of Tolstoy's "postconversion" thought, they have their roots in the reflections of his youth. Perhaps the briefest summary of the content of *On Life* would be that each person has two lives—a spiritual life (the more important) and a physical life (the less important); each person's task is to understand this and to live so that the less important, physical life will be in conformity with the requirements of the more important, spiritual life; this means that the law of the physical life—to seek the well-being of the flesh—must be supplanted by the law of the spiritual life—to seek the well-being of others. This conclusion can be found already in Tolstoy's youthful diary, in which he once copied out the maxim (whether his own or another's is not clear) "The desire of the flesh is one's own good; the desire of the soul is the good of others."

As we consider the relevance of *On Life* for a reading of *The Death of Ivan Ilich*, then, it is clear from the outset that besides a rather strange biographical coincidence marking Tolstoy's original impulse to begin to think through the content of *On Life*, there is also general agreement between the main thoughts of that book and the conclusions to which Ivan Ilich comes in the last days and hours of his life. This by no means, however, exhausts the points of contact between the two works, as we shall see when we examine *On Life* in more detail. I will divide this examination of *On Life* according to the specific points of thematic contact it makes with *The Death of Ivan Ilich*.

The Divided Self One of Tolstoy's main concerns in *On Life* is to provide a reasoned account of human nature, a sort of essential and generalized anthropology. His account is to the effect that each individual human being exists in two separate yet interrelated modes. Each person possesses a material, physiological life (what Tolstoy calls the person's "animal personality," the flesh), which coexists with an immaterial, spiritual life (which he refers to as the person's "human personality," the spirit). In Tolstoy's account, the physiological life of the human being, because it is visibly and tangibly present to the individual, often conceals the existence of the immaterial, spiritual life. However, Tolstoy is confident that a moment comes in the life of each person when the physiological self begins to sense the presence of its companion self. Tolstoy puts it this way: "In observing the manifestation of life in a human being, we see that true life is always preserved in a person in the same way as it is preserved in a seed, and the time comes when this life reveals itself" (26:345). He goes on to develop the comparison between the seed and the person, describing how the seed breaks and the life within it burgeons forth.

At this point, according to *On Life*, a divarication (or division) of the self begins to occur, and the individual becomes aware that she or he is two personalities, rather than one. Tolstoy speaks of the existence of two competing "I's": one, the physiological personality; the other, the reason (26:340).

This divarication of the previously contented self is perceived by the self at first as a source of discomfort (as something "diseased" and "unnatural" [26:344]), later with pangs of suffering, and finally as a phenomenon that has "poisoned his life" (26:340). Tolstoy represents the tension between these two "I's" as a discussion between them, as though they were engaged in a debate. For example, in chapter 19 of *On Life* we read: " 'But this is not life,' responds the confused, lost human consciousness. 'This is a renunciation of life, suicide.'... 'I know nothing of that,' answers the rational consciousness. 'I know only that that which you call your pleasures are good for you only when you do not take them for yourself, but receive them from others.'... 'But I know life only in my own personality. It is impossible for me to put my life into the good of other beings' " (26:371–73).

Ivan Ilich in the novel begins to engage in conversations with the voice of his soul in very much the same way. These debates suggest to him that his life, as he has lived it, has been wrong, and, just as stubbornly as the physiological consciousness in *On Life*, the voice of Ivan Ilich's formerly contented self denies this conclusion.

Space and Time In the epigraph to *On Life*, Tolstoy included famous passages from the works of two noted philosophers: Blaise Pascal and Immanuel Kant (26:313). The passage from Pascal, his celebrated "Man is only a reed, . . . but a thinking reed," mentions the concepts of space and time directly, saying that it is not they that provide the essential parameters of human life, but rather the capacity of the human being to think. Kant, of course, is renowned for his idea that space and time have their existence as categories of the human understanding. The point of both, it would seem, is to suggest that space and time are not the determinative factors they appear to common sense to be.

Our analysis of *The Death of Ivan Ilich* (see especially chapter 9 of this book) has suggested that Tolstoy structured the novel in such a way that in the world represented on the novel's surface space and time are presented as determinative of the life course of the protagonist; in fact, on the surface level of the novel, the death of the protagonist coincides with the completion of the process of the shrinkage of the space and time available to him in his life. It is at this very moment of the ending of time and space, however, that Ivan Ilich (or at least that inward part of him whose reflections Tolstoy had been carefully following throughout the last four chapters of the novel) senses that he has entered a space without dimensions and an instant that would never change (167 [26:113]). *The Death of Ivan Ilich* represents in narrative and images a point that Tolstoy would later make explicit in *On Life*: the falseness of the teaching that "life is the period of time between birth and death" (26:341). Also in *On Life*, Tolstoy glosses the "life of the animal personality" as "spatial, temporal life" (26:360) and the true "human [spiritual] life" of the individual is said to be immune to the "limitations of space and time" (26:361). The Russian word for "limitation" (*predel*) is also employed prominently in the description of the young and rising Ivan Ilich in the novel. He is said to be a person assured of a good career and material success in part because he always knows where the "limits" (*predely*) of social propriety lie and never oversteps them (130 [26:70]). *On Life*, then, contains an explicit discussion of the idea that the "true life" of a human being is not dependent on the exigencies of the physical body in space and time. We have seen this same idea worked out in narrative and image in *The Death of Ivan Ilich*.

Reversal In chapter 9 of this book I discussed at some length the various patterns of reversal Tolstoy incorporates into the structure of *The Death of Ivan Ilich*. An interesting parallel can be found in *On Life*. In comparing the human being's dawning awareness of the true life hidden within the physiological life to the germination of a seed, Tolstoy describes the husk of the seed, the part that dies in order that the life within might come forth, by using the word *obolochka* ("surrounding edge," "cover") (26:347). This, as it happens, is the same word used in the description of Ivan Ilich in his coffin in chapter 1 of the novel, where the dead, but significant, face of Ivan Ilich is framed by the *obolochka* of the coffin. The husk (the *obolochka*) of the seed, in Tolstoy's analogy, represents the physiological life of the individual; in the novel, the dead body of Ivan Ilich is also associated with this word. Thus, the ordinary "life" of the individual is represented as in fact his death. Here the significance of an image used in the novel may be better understood by viewing it from the perspective afforded by *On Life*. In any case, in *On Life* Tolstoy makes the falseness of the claim of the physiological life as the true life of a person completely unambiguous: "[physiological] existence is slow death" (26:347).

Another obvious reversal in the novel is that of the meanings of health and disease. It is the disease that afflicts the body of Ivan Ilich that leads ultimately to the recovered health of his soul. The attendant implication is that health of the body would suggest a sickness of the spirit. It is clear that Tolstoy has used health and disease in the novel in a highly symbolic fashion and through this usage has emphasized the tension between the physiological and spiritual planes of human existence. Tolstoy expressed this incompatibility directly in *On Life*: "The true life of a person . . . begins only when the renunciation of the good of the animal personality commences" (26:347), or again: "death [i.e., the death of the animal personality] is the entrance into the new relationship to the world" (26:409).

Death and Birth *The Death of Ivan Ilich* is replete with images of death and descriptions of dying, but it contains as well many allusions to birth. Our earlier analysis has pointed out the pain and trauma of Ivan Ilich's passage from the darkness into the light, the image of the "black bag," the rapidly increasing tempo of the novel's ever shorter chapters, and the comparison between the behavior of Ivan Ilich in his illness with that of his wife during her pregnancy as details in the novel that might be read as birth allusions. If they are read this way, then it seems clear that the "death" of Ivan Ilich in the last chapter of the novel also represents his birth (or his rebirth) into life. This reading of the novel is certainly congruent with Tolstoy's affirmation in *On Life* of the incompatibility of the false, physiological life of the human being and the true, spiritual life; as we have seen, Tolstoy goes so far as to say that the possession of the one is dependent on the loss of the other. At one point in *On Life* Tolstoy even compares death and birth with one another: "The great change in your condition which death will bring terrifies you; but don't forget that just such a great change happened to you at your birth as well" (26:418). In this case, Tolstoy's representation of this theme in fiction is more daring than its philosophical presentation. In *On Life* he merely compares the trauma of death with that of birth; in the novel he has used death as a realized metaphor for birth, has shown not simply that death is like birth but is, in fact, a form of birth.

At the end of *The Death of Ivan Ilich* the reader is left with the conviction that although the protagonist has died in the physiological sense, he has overcome death in the spiritual sense. We have seen that the flesh is determined by space and time and that the novel is so arranged as to show a gradual diminishment of both as Ivan's biography progresses. At the end Ivan Ilich runs out of space and time, but at the same moment, in the spiritual sense, he escapes from their bondage. In *On Life* the title of chapter 28 expresses the same theme explicitly: "The death of the flesh destroys the spatial body and the temporal consciousness, but cannot destroy that which comprises the [true] basis of life" (26:401). The true life of the spirit is said in *On Life* to be unassailable by death, so that from the spiritual point of view death is a chimera. What is real, according to *On Life* is the fear of death (26:406), an affirmation that, as we have seen, was frequently made in *The Death of Ivan Ilich*.

Alienation We have observed in *The Death of Ivan Ilich* a studied use of images of isolation to portray the protagonist's gradually increasing sense of alienation from those around him. We have seen that in the final chapter of the novel, Ivan Ilich realizes that he has been responsible for his separation from other people, that by his own choices he has come to the point of being all alone. The reading of the novel offered in this book has shown that Ivan Ilich responded to any situation or relationship that was not conductive to a pleasant and "proper" life by distancing himself from it. This pattern of behavior suggests the underlying conviction that only the self has value and that other people exist only to the extent that they play a favorable or unfavorable role in the self's attempt to achieve a pleasant life. In *On Life*, this attitude is described explicitly and defined as the condition in which a person whose spiritual self yet lies dormant is confined: "A person lives and acts only to obtain the good for himself, to produce the result that all people and even all beings would live and act only to the end of his obtaining that good, so that he would have pleasure, and so that for him there would be neither suffering nor death" (26:369).

Of course, as the novel shows, the approach to the good in life by means of selfishness leads only to a dead end of never-quite-fulfilled desires. No matter to what new heights Ivan Ilich aspires or to what new levels his salary grows, he always remains "a couple of thousand rubles short." In distancing himself as he does from those around him, he forecloses his only chance of achieving the genuine good of life. The only salvation for the hopelessly alienated individual is the purposeful reestablishment of the relationships that the individual, in the selfish quest for happiness, has ruptured. In chapter 12 of the novel, Ivan Ilich's climactic moment of illumination is simultaneous with the accidental contact of his hand with the top of his son's head. In our analysis this was construed as a metaphor for the reestablishment of his connection with those around him, as a breaking down of the screens that Ivan Ilich had erected around himself in his lonely quest for the good life. Once he has broken out of his alienation Ivan Ilich is no longer overwhelmed by the pain of his illness; in fact, he becomes distanced from it, observing it as though it pertained to another rather than to himself. His concern is now for others, his son and his formerly despised wife, rather than for himself. Once again we see this idea expressed directly in *On Life*:

> A person's animal personality demands the good, but rational consciousness shows the person the poverty of all those beings struggling with one another, shows him that there can be no good for the animal personality. . . . And then . . . the person finds in his soul a feeling which gives him that very good to which his rational consciousness had been directing him. And this feeling not only resolves the former contradiction of life but, as it were, finds in this contradiction itself the motivation for the discovery of this feeling. Animal personalities want to make use of the animal personality to obtain their own ends. But the feeling of love leads a person to give up his own existence for the benefit of other beings. (26:383)

Health and Disease In our analysis of *The Death of Ivan Ilich* we arrived at the conclusion that health and disease function in the novel both as phenomena of physiological life and as metaphors for the condition of the protagonist's spiritual being. It is certainly true that

Ivan Ilich is really and physically ill, but (as he often observes) the worst sufferings he is forced to endure are spiritual rather than physiological. From this point of view, the novel represents not merely the suffering of one who has, by ill luck, been stricken with a painfully terminal disease, but also the suffering inherent in the life of each person who remains locked in the alienation characteristic of what Tolstoy, in *On Life*, calls the animal personality. The description Tolstoy provides of such a person in *On Life* is highly reminiscent of Ivan Ilich: "Such a person [i.e., one not yet awakened to the spiritual dimension of life] sees death before himself/herself constantly, and nothing can save her/him from it. With every day and hour the position of such a person becomes worse and worse, and nothing can be done to make it better" (26:410).

Suffering In *The Death of Ivan Ilich* it is the pain and suffering occasioned by the protagonist's illness that drives him gradually to an awareness of the wrongness of his former mode of life. His path to enlightenment is made difficult by his attachment to the idea that his life had been good, appropriate, virtuous. The implication of the novel would seem to be that if suffering functions as a reminder or guide to those who yet remain spiritually dormant, as a motivation to them to continue to seek spiritual wisdom, then the discomfort, the dis-ease, will have to be all the greater if a person who is convinced of the goodness and propriety of the life currently led is to be brought to see the flaws in that life and to embark upon a revised understanding of his/her relationship with the surrounding world. In Ivan Ilich's case the greatest hindrance to any new understanding of life is his perception of the inexplicability and, above all, the injustice of his suffering. As we have seen so often already in the preceding pages, *On Life* contains an explicit rationalization of this theme also. Tolstoy explores his nascent awareness that life as he has understood it may not in fact be able to supply all the rewards and gratification he desires from it. "I am engaged in a good calling, one which is without doubt of use to other people, and suddenly I am seized by illness; it disrupts my calling and exhausts me and tortures me without any sense or meaning" (26:423). This is only one of several examples of unexpected and unjustified suffering that Tolstoy introduces at this point in *On Life*, but it is clearly one that has a special significance for readers of *The Death of Ivan Ilich*.

In *On Life* Tolstoy makes explicit the idea that suffering and pain may be seen as physiological analogues of spiritual discomforts. He seems occasionally to verge on the ascription of all suffering to the shortcomings of the individual's spiritual awareness, that is, to sin. In the novel, the relationships between the health of the body and the sickness of the soul and between the death of the body and the birth of the soul remain at the level of powerful metaphors. It is nowhere characteristic of the novel to pass over into the kind of straightforward, and sometimes grossly oversimplified, explanations that are to be found in *On Life*. And yet it seems clear that *On Life* can be used as an index and gloss to a variety of the themes in the novel. Despite the apparent similarity of thematic concerns between the two works, however, the good reader will not want to go so far as to reduce the novel to a recapitulation of those themes.

This chapter has shown that in other works written about the same time as *The Death of Ivan Ilich* Tolstoy concerned himself with the philosophical discussion and resolution of the tension between the competing forces of matter and spirit in human life. His task in the novel was evidently the same, and the sense of freedom in the spirit and the "true understanding of life" is perhaps more effectively expressed in the allusive, symbolic, and structurally complex medium of *The Death of Ivan Ilich* (or *Master and Man*) than in the reasoned simplicity of *On Life* or *The Gospel in Brief*.

NOTES AND REFERENCES

Chapter 1

1. I use this term, apparently first coined by the philosopher Gottfried Leibniz, following the example of Guy de Mallac, who has been kind enough to share with me his unpublished monograph on Tolstoy's philosophy.

2. Lev Tolstoi, *Polnoe sobranie sochinenii* (Moscow and Leningrad: Gosudarstvennoe Izdatel'stvo Khudozhestvennoi Literatury, 1928–58), vol. 23, 32. References to the Russian originals of Tolstoy's works, including letters, are to those works as published in this, the "Jubilee Edition" of Tolstoy's complete collected works. All translations from the Russian are my own, except those from the text of *The Death of Ivan Ilich*. Hereafter, all references to the Russian originals of Tolstoy's works will be given parenthetically in the text in the form "(volume number:page number)"; thus, the present reference would be "(23:32)."

3. On a business trip in that year to the small town of Arzamas Tolstoy was obliged to pass the night in a hotel and was there, in the wee hours of the morning, overcome for the first time by a personal sense of the futility of life and the dreadful inevitability of death.

4. As early as the middle of the 1850s Tolstoy had expressed the belief that Christianity would provide a viable philosophy of life were it relieved of the insupportable weight of its theology and dogma. Still earlier, as he later recalled, he had dramatically thrown away the icon that the Orthodox commonly wore upon their necks in favor of a medallion engraved with the face of Jean-Jacques Rousseau.

Chapter 2

1. Matthew Arnold, "Count Leo Tolstoi," *Fortnightly Review* (December, 1887). Reprinted in A. V. Knowles, ed., *Tolstoy: The Critical Heritage* (London: Routledge and Kegan Paul, 1978), 353.

Chapter 3

1. The novel was first published in volume 12 of the *Compositions of Count L. N. Tolstoy* (*Sochineniia grafa L. N. Tolstogo*), which was published in April 1886.

2. N. K. Mikhailovskii, *Sobranie sochinenii*, vol. 6 (St. Petersburg, 1897), 382. Cited in L. D. Opul'skaia, *Lev Nikolaevich Tolstoi: Materialy k biografii s 1886 po 1892 god* (Moscow: Izdatel'stvo "Nauka," 1979), 14; hereafter cited as Opul'skaia.

3. Lisovsky's remarks appeared in the journal *Russkoe bogatstvo*, 1888, no. 1:182. Cited in Opul'skaia, 15.

4. This book, published in France in the mid-1880s, was a crucial factor in the dawning awareness of European intellectuals of the excellence of the Russian literary culture.

5. One exception that should be noted is Edward Wasiolek's, "Tolstoy's *The Death of Ivan Ilyich* and Jamesian Fictional Imperatives," *Modern Fiction Studies* 6(1960):314–24; hereafter cited in text as Wasiolek. This essay disputes the validity of criticism directed at the overtly moralizing tone of the novel. Wasiolek finds the basis of this criticism in the assumptions and presuppositions of a Jamesian aesthetic of indirection and suggests a rejoinder along the lines of taking Tolstoy on his own, rather than another's, aesthetic terms.

6. D. D. Blagoi et al., eds., *Istoriia russkoi literatury v trekh tomakh*, vol. 3 (Moscow: Izdatel'stvo "Nauka," 1964), 575.

7. See especially Boris Sorokin, "Ivan Il'ich as Jonah: A Cruel Joke," *Canadian Slavic Studies* 5 (1971): 487–88, 490; hereafter cited in text as Sorokin; Philip Rahv, "*The Death of Ivan Illych* and Joseph K.," in *Image and Idea: Twenty Essays on Literary Themes* (Norfolk, Conn.: New Directions, 1957), 135; and William Barrett, "Existentialism as a Symptom of Man's Contemporary Crisis," in *Spiritual Problems in Contemporary Literature*, ed. Stanley Hopper (New York: Harper, 1952), 143.

8. Lev Shestov, "The Last Judgment: Tolstoy's Last Works," in *In Job's Balances: On the Sources of the Eternal Truths* (Athens: Ohio University Press, 1957), 117; hereafter cited in text as Shestov.

9. William B. Edgerton, "Tolstoy, Immortality, and Twentieth-Century Physics," *Canadian Slavonic Papers* 21(1979):300; hereafter cited in text as Edgerton.

10. A number of studies of this type appeared; they generally concluded that some form of cancer was the proper diagnosis.

11. James Bartell, "The Trauma of Birth in *The Death of Ivan Ilych*: A Therapeutic Reading," *Psychological Review* 2(1978): 106–11.

12. Y. J. Dayananda, "*The Death of Ivan Ilych*: A Psychological Study On Death and Dying," *Literature and Psychology* 22(1972): 192–97.

13. Charles I. Glicksberg, "Tolstoy and *The Death of Ivan Illyitch*," in

Notes and References

The Ironic Vision in Modern Literature (Hague: Martinus Nijhoff, 1969):82–83; hereafter cited in text as Glicksberg.

14. Geoffrey Clive, "Tolstoy and the Varieties of the Inauthentic," in *The Broken Icon: Intuitive Existentialism in Classical Russian Fiction* (New York: Macmillan, 1970), 108–12; hereafter cited in text as Clive.

15. James Olney, "Experience, Metaphor, and Meaning: *The Death of Ivan Ilych*," *Journal of Aesthetics and Art Criticism* 31(1972):113; hereafter cited in text as Olney.

16. Irving Halperin, "The Structural Integrity of *The Death of Ivan Il'ich*," *Slavic and East European Journal* 5(1961):337; hereafter cited in the text as Halperin.

17. John Donnelly, "Death and Ivan Ilych," in *Language, Metaphysics, and Death*, ed. John Donnelly (New York: Fordham University Press, 1978), 118.

18. A notable exception is Gunter Schaarschmidt's study of the syntax of the novel, which, though written by a linguist, suggests important conclusions on the artistic structure of the work ("Theme and Discourse Structure in *The Death of Ivan Il'ich*," *Canadian Slavonic Papers* 21(1979):356–66; hereafter cited in text as Schaarschmidt).

19. George Gutsche, in fact, devotes the last part of his chapter on *The Death of Ivan Ilich* to disputing the extent of the relevance of Tolstoy's formal religious ideas for an interpretation of the novel (*Moral Apostasy in Russian Literature* [DeKalb: Northern Illinois University Press, 1986]).

20. Richard F. Gustafson, *Leo Tolstoy: Resident and Stranger* (Princeton, N.J.: Princeton University Press, 1986), 155–60.

21. C. J. G. Turner, "The Language of Fiction: Word Cluster in Tolstoy's *The Death of Ivan Ilych*," *Modern Language Review* 65(1970):121, hereafter cited in text as Turner.

22. David Matual, "*The Confession* as Subtext in *The Death of Ivan Ilich*," *International Fiction Review* 8(1981):125–28; hereafter cited in text as Matual.

23. Art, for the symbolists, involved the portrayal of *realia* (the real) in the interest of leading our attention to *realiora* (the more real, the essence of existence).

24. Rima Salys, "Signs on the Road of Life: *The Death of Ivan Il'ich*," *Slavic and East European Journal* 30(1986):18–28.

Chapter 4

1. T. A. Kuzminskaia, *Moia zhizn' doma i v Iasnoi Poliane*, 3d ed. (Tula, 1958), 446.

2. See Gary R. Jahn, "The Unity of *Anna Karenina*," *The Russian Review* 41(1982):144–58.

Chapter 5

1. The call of judgment is implicit in the final lines of chapter 1. Peter Ivanovich "did not once look at the corpse" during the memorial service and "to the very end of it did not give way to its enervating influences." There follows a brief exchange between Peter Ivanovich and Gerasim: " 'Well, brother Gerasim . . . it's too bad, isn't it?' 'It's God's will. We'll all come to it.' " Peter Ivanovich manages to ignore even so direct a hint as this, however, and departs in high spirits, thinking of a game of cards and enjoying the "fresh air" after "the smell of incense, the corpse, and carbolic acid" (129 [26:68]).

Chapter 6

1. It is worth noting that Tolstoy lists the things that "upset" Ivan Ilich; the first two mentioned are "an unpleasantness with his wife" and "a mishap at work" (143[26:86]). Thus Tolstoy reminds us of Ivan Ilich's history of dealing with disruptions in the pleasant flow of life and suggests that his illness is comparable to the situation he faced when his wife was pregnant and when he was passed over for promotion.

Chapter 8

1. The awfulness of Ivan Ilich's suffering has sometimes been criticized as excessive, given that he is portrayed as an "ordinary" rather than an "evil" person. See Wasiolek for a discussion of this point.

Chapter 9

1. Mark Aldanov, *Zagadka Tolstogo* (Berlin: 1923; Providence, R. I.: Brown University Press, 1969), 60.

2. Tolstoy made frequent use of the motif of a change or confusion in direction. In the "Introduction" to *What I Believe* (*V chem moja vera*, 1884), for example, he wrote, in describing his own "conversion," that "it happened to me as it happens to a man who goes out on some business and on the way suddenly decides that the business is unnecessary and returns home. All that was on his right is now on his left, and all that was on his left is now on his

right; his former wish to get as far as possible from home has changed into a wish to be as near as possible to it. The direction of my life and desires became different, and good and evil changed places" (23:8).

3. The motifs of Ivan as a child and the comforts of childhood are introduced as early as chapter 7, e.g., Ivan's childish helplessness and his desire to be pampered and cared for as by a mother. The role of nursemaid is fulfilled by the uncomplaining Gerasim.

Chapter 10

1. The theme "Tolstoy and death" is a familiar one in the literature. Of special interest are Janko Lavrin, *Tolstoy: An Approach* (New York: Macmillan, 1946), 81–93; D. Y. Kvitko, *A Philosophical Study of Tolstoy* (New York, 1927), especially chapter 1, section 4; and G. W. Spence, *Tolstoy the Ascetic* (London: Oliver and Boyd, 1967).

2. The feeling that the death of another implies the reality of one's own death is also keenly experienced by Levin in *Anna Karenina* (see his meeting with his dying brother, Nikolai [17:367–68]).

3. This notion is nowhere more succinctly expressed by Tolstoy than in chapter 6 of *The Death of Ivan Ilich* wherein is described the attitude of the protagonist toward the exemplary syllogism given in Kiesewetter's *Logic*: Caius is a man, all men are mortal, therefore Caius is mortal (149 [26:92–93]).

4. *The Gospel in Brief* is a condensation of *A Harmonization and Translation of the Four Gospels*; first published in 1883, it contains Tolstoy's translation of the Gospel texts.

5. Quoted in the "Commentary" to *On Life* (26:748).

6. Quoted in the "Commentary" to *On Life* (26:748).

7. There have been translations of this work into English (e.g., that in *The Oxford Centenary Edition of the Works of Leo Tolstoy*, ed. A. Maude [London: Oxford University Press, 1930]), but they are not always readily available. In this book I translate directly from the original Russian text (26:311–442).

8. The most complete treatment of Tolstoy's dualism is found in G. W. Spence's *Tolstoy the Ascetic* (London: Oliver and Boyd, 1967).

SELECTED BIBLIOGRAPHY

Primary Works

Polnoe sobranie sochinenii v devianosto tomakh. 90 vols. Moscow and Leningrad: Gosudarstvennoe Izdatel'stvo Khudozhestvennoi Literatury, 1928–1958. Called the "Jubilee Edition" because its publication commenced on the one hundredth anniversary of Tolstoy's birth, this is the standard scholarly edition of Tolstoy's works. It contains printed and manuscript variants, supplemented by introductions to and commentary on the texts. In addition, it contains the most complete collection of Tolstoy's letters, diaries, notebooks, and other personal papers. Text of and commentary on *The Death of Ivan Ilich* (Russian title, *Smert' Ivana Il'icha*) is in volume 26 of this edition.

The Death of Ivan Ilich. In *Tolstoy's Short Fiction,* edited and with revised translations by Michael R. Katz, 123–67. New York: W. W. Norton & Co., 1991. Of the many translations of *The Death of Ivan Ilich* currently available, this edition, originally translated by Louise and Aylmer Maude, provides the best text for study. It provides a translation of the text by persons who were closely acquainted with Tolstoy and who had the benefit of his advice with respect to the translation of difficult passages. Their work has been further improved by the revisions of the editor. This edition also contains a helpful supplement of scholarly materials, including extracts from Tolstoy's personal papers and letters, a selection of scholarly articles on Tolstoy's short fiction, a chronology of his life and works, and a selected bibliography.

Tolstoy's Letters, edited and translated by R. F. Christian. 2 vols. New York: Charles Scribner's Sons, 1978.

Tolstoy's Diaries, edited and translated by R. F. Christian. 2 vols. New York: Scribner Press, 1985.

Secondary Works

Barrett, William. "Existentialism as a Symptom of Man's Contemporary Crisis." In *Spiritual Problems in Contemporary Literature*, edited by Stanley Hopper, 139–52. New York: Harper, 1952. Brief discussion of the novel as exemplary of the spiritual emptiness of modern life.

Bartell, James. "The Trauma of Birth in *The Death of Ivan Ilych*: A Therapeutic Reading." *Psychological Review* 2(1978): 97–117. The novel discussed from the vantage point of certain schemes of psychotherapy.

Borker, David. "Sentential Structure in Tolstoy's *Smert' Ivana Il'icha*." In *American Contributions to the VIII International Congress of Slavists: Linguistics and Poetics*, edited by H. Birnbaum, vol. 1, 180–95. Columbus, Ohio: Slavica, 1978. A linguistic analysis of the sentence structure of the novel.

Cain, T. G. S. *Tolstoy*. New York: Barnes & Noble, 1977. A general life and works of Tolstoy; contains a chapter on the novel.

Carr, Arthur C. *The Death of Ivan Illych*. New York: Health Sciences Publishing Corporation, 1973.

Cate, Hollis L. "On Death and Dying in Tolstoy's *The Death of Ivan Ilyich*." *Hartford Studies in Literature* 7(1975):195–205. Discussion of the novel in the context of modern discussions of the stages of dying and death.

Christian, R. F. *Tolstoy: A Critical Introduction*. Cambridge: Cambridge University Press, 1969. The standard life and works of Tolstoy in English; contains a solid and circumspect discussion of the novel.

Clive, Geoffrey. "Tolstoy and the Varieties of the Inauthentic." In *The Broken Icon: Intuitive Existentialism in Classical Russian Fiction*, 86–127. New York: Macmillan, 1970. Approaches the novel as a portrait of a spiritually and emotionally empty life.

Dayananda, Y. J. "*The Death of Ivan Ilych*: A Psychological Study *On Death and Dying*." *Literature and Psychology* 22 (1972): 191–98. The most complete discussion of the novel as a fictional precursor to modern discussions of the stages of dying and death.

Donnelly, John. "Death and Ivan Ilych." In *Language, Metaphysics, and Death*, edited by J. Donnelly, 116–30. New York: Fordham University Press, 1978. The novel is used as a point of departure for the author's own philosophical reflections.

Edel, Leon. "Portrait of the Artist as an Old Man." In *Aging, Death, and the Completion of Being*, edited by David D. Van Tassel, 193–214. Philadelphia: University of Pennsylvania Press, 1979.

Edgerton, William B. "Tolstoy, Immortality, and Twentieth-Century Physics."

Canadian Slavonic Papers 21(1979) :300ff. A seminal contribution to the discussion of patterns of reversal in the novel.

Glicksberg, Charles I. "Tolstoy and *The Death of Ivan Illyitch*." In his *The Ironic Vision in Modern Literature*, 81–86. Hague: Nijhoff, 1969.

Gubler, Donworth V. "A Study of Illness and Death in the Lives and Representative Works of Leo Tolstoy and Thomas Mann." Ph.D. diss. Brigham Young University. Summary in *Dissertation Abstracts International*, vol. 32, p. 4000A.

Gustafson, Richard F. *Leo Tolstoy: Resident and Stranger*. Princeton, N.J.: Princeton University Press, 1986. A very important book on Tolstoy; based firmly in an extensive knowledge of Tolstoy's diaries, letters, and nonfictional writings; the most complete modern treatment of the relationship between Tolstoy and the established church.

Gustafson, Richard F. "The Three Stages of Man." *Canadian-American Slavic Studies* 12(1978):481–518.

Gutsche, George. *Moral Apostasy in Russian Literature*. DeKalb, Ill.: Northern Illinois University Press, 1986. Contains a chapter on the novel, providing an excellent synthesis of previous scholarship and an original view of the novel, particularly of the psychology of the protagonist.

Halperin, Irving. "The Structural Integrity of *The Death of Ivan Il'ich*." *Slavic and East European Journal* 5(1961): 334–40. One of the first studies to point out the significance of the novel's organization and structure.

Hirschberg, W. R. "Tolstoy's *The Death of Ivan Illych*." *Explicator* 28(1969), no. 3, item 26.

Howe, Irving. "Leo Tolstoy: *The Death of Ivan Illych*." In *Classics of Modern Fiction*, 113–78. New York: Harcourt Brace Jovanovich, 1972.

Jahn, Gary R. "*The Death of Ivan Il'ich*—Chapter One." In *Studies in Nineteenth and Twentieth Century Polish and Russian Literature in Honor of Xenia Gasiorowska*, 37–43. Columbus, Ohio: Slavica Publishers, 1983. Discussion of the placement of the first chapter in violation of the novel's predominantly chronological organization.

Jahn, Gary R. "A Note on the Miracle Motifs in the Later Works of Lev Tolstoj." In *The Supernatural in Slavic and Baltic Literatures: Essays in Honor of Victor Terras*, 191–99. Columbus, Ohio: Slavica Publishers, 1988. Discussion of the references to the crucifixion of Jesus in the novel.

Jahn, Gary R. "The Role of the Ending in Lev Tolstoi's *The Death of Ivan Il'ich*." *Canadian Slavonic Papers* 24(1982):229–38. Discussion of patterns of reversal, structural considerations, and multiple levels of significance in the novel.

Matual, David. " 'The Confession' as Subtext in *The Death of Ivan Ilich*." *International Fiction Review* 8(1981):121–30. Discussion of the connection between the novel and Tolstoy's earlier work *A Confession*.

Selected Bibliography

Olney, James. "Experience, Metaphor, and Meaning: *The Death of Ivan Iliych*. *Journal of Aesthetics and Art Criticism* 31(1972):101–14. An important contribution to the discussion of the use of symbol and metaphor in the novel.

Pachmuss, Temira. "The Theme of Love and Death in Tolstoy's *The Death of Ivan Ilych*." *American Slavic and East European Review* 20(1961):72–83.

Parthé, Kathleen. "The Metamorphosis of Death in Tolstoy." *Language and Style* 18(1985):205–14. Further discussion of Tolstoy's attempts to deal with his own deeply rooted fear of death.

Parthé, Kathleen. "Tolstoy and the Geometry of Fear." *Modern Language Studies* 15(1985):480–92. A discussion of Tolstoy's attitudes toward death as shown in the novel and in other works.

Rahv, Philip. "*The Death of Ivan Illych* and Joseph K." In *Image and Idea: Twenty Essays on Literary Themes*, 121–40. Norfolk, Conn.: New Directions, 1957. Discussion of the comparability between the novel and Kafka's *The Trial*.

Raleigh, John Henry. "Tolstoy and Sight: The Dual Nature of Reality." *Essays in Criticism: A Quarterly Journal of Literary Criticism* 21:170–79.

Reichbart, Richard. "Psi Phenomena and Tolstoi." *Journal of the American Society for Psychological Research* 70(1976):249–65.

Russell, Robert. "From Individual to Universal: Tolstoy's *Smert' Ivana Il'icha*." *Modern Language Review* 76(1981):629–42. Discussion of the means employed by Tolstoy to "globalize" the experience of the protagonist.

Salys, Rima. "Signs on the Road of Life: *The Death of Ivan Il'ich*." *Slavic and East European Journal* 30(1986):18–28. An excellent, detailed study of metaphor in the novel, especially the covert significance of foreign language phrases.

Schaarschmidt, Gunter. "Theme and Discourse Structure in *The Death of Ivan Il'ich*." *Canadian Slavonic Papers* 21(1979):356–66. Commentary on the organization of the novel and of the interface between theme and organization.

Schefski, Harold K. "Tolstoj's Case Against Doctors." *Slavic and East European Journal* 22(1978):569–73. Information on Tolstoy's attitude toward the medical profession.

Shestov, Lev. *The Good in the Teaching of Tolstoy and Nietzsche: Philosophy and Preaching*. Athens: Ohio University Press, 1969.

Shestov, Lev. "The Last Judgement: Tolstoy's Last Works. In *Job's Balances: On the Sources of the Eternal Truths*, 83–138. Athens: Ohio University Press, 1957. An important reading of Tolstoy by a contemporary and one of the founders of existentialist thought.

Smyrniew, Walter. "Tolstoy's Depiction of Death in the Context of Recent Studies of the Experience of Dying." *Canadian Slavonic Papers* 21(1979):376–79.

Sorokin, Boris. "Ivan Il'ich as Jonah: A Cruel Joke." *Canadian Slavic Studies* 5(1971):487–507. A thought-provoking analysis of certain aspects of the symbolism of the novel.

Speirs, Logan. "Tolstoy and Chekhov: *The Death of Ivan Ilych* and *A Dreary Story*." *Oxford Review* 8(1968):81–93.

Turner, C. J. G. "The Language of Fiction: Word Cluster in Tolstoy's *The Death of Ivan Ilych*." *Modern Language Review* 65(1970):116–21. Discussion of the placement of the first chapter of the novel.

Wasiolek, Edward. *Tolstoy's Major Fiction*. Chicago: University of Chicago Press, 1978. Discussion of Tolstoy's most important works; contains a chapter on the novel.

Wasiolek, Edward. "Tolstoy's *The Death of Ivan Ilyich* and Jamesian Fictional Imperatives." *Modern Fiction Studies* 6(1960):314–24. A discussion of the possible strategies that might be followed in reading the novel.

Wexelblatt, Robert. "The Higher Parody: Ivan Ilych's Metamorphosis and the Death of Gregor Samsa." *Massachusetts Review* 21(1980):601–28. Comparison of the novel to Kafka's story "The Metamorphosis."

INDEX

113

Index

The Author

Gary R. Jahn is Associate Professor of Russian Language and Literature in the Department of Slavic and Central Asian Languages and Literatures at the University of Minnesota. He previously taught at St. Olaf College in Northfield, Minnesota, and at the State University of New York at Buffalo. Professor Jahn is the author of numerous articles on various aspects of Tolstoy's literary career, especially his aesthetic views and his novels *Anna Karenina* and *The Death of Ivan Ilich*.